D0120138

2016

A NEW PROCLAMATION FOR A NEW GENERATION

GERARD O'NEILL

MERCIER PRESS

Irish Publisher – Irish Story

MERCIER PRESS
Cork
www.mercierpress.ie

Trade enquiries to CMD BookSource,
55a Spruce Avenue, Stillorgan Industrial Park,
Blackrock, County Dublin

© Gerard O'Neill, 2010

ISBN: 978 1 85635 690 9

10 9 8 7 6 5 4 3 2 1

A CIP record for this title is available from the British Library

This book is sold subject to the condition that it shall not, by way of trade or
otherwise, be lent, resold, hired out or otherwise circulated without the publisher's
prior consent in any form of binding or cover other than that in which it is published
and without a similar condition including this condition being imposed on the
subsequent purchaser.

No part of this publication may be reproduced or transmitted in any form or by
any means, electronic or mechanical, including photocopying, recording or any
information or retrieval system, without the prior permission of the publisher in
writing.

Printed and bound by ScandBook AB, Sweden.

Contents

To my parents, Gerard and Marie, for my past

To my wife, Gráinne, for my present

To my children, Emmet and Hannah, for my future.

Acknowledgements

The idea for this book originated in a bar. I even have witnesses – Damian Devaney, Tom Trainor and Matt Kavanagh – with whom I was discussing the future of Irish marketing at the time. As we debated the wider context of Ireland's future, it struck me that what we needed was a '2016 Proclamation' – one that would inspire a new generation to forge a better future. So I took it upon myself to have a go at doing just that: preparing a first draft of a 2016 proclamation, informed by a re-evaluation of the content and consequences of the 1916 Proclamation.

As with the initial inspiration, I have others to thank for the final outcome of this book. I would like to thank the members of the '2016 Club' for their feedback and support, including Liam Sheehan and Paul Cooke. And I would especially like to thank Barre Fitzpatrick and Michael McLoughlin for their invaluable commentary and suggestions regarding an earlier draft of this book. I also owe a big debt of gratitude to my colleagues at Amárach Research, especially in relation to the 2016 survey that explored some of the themes of this book.

And finally I would like to thank Mary Feehan, Patrick Crowley and Wendy Logue at Mercier Press for their enthusiasm, commitment and editing support without which this book would not have been possible.

POBLACHT NA H EIREANN.

THE PROVISIONAL GOVERNMENT
OF THE
IRISH REPUBLIC
TO THE PEOPLE OF IRELAND.

IRISHMEN AND IRISHWOMEN : In the name of God and of the dead generations from which she receives her old tradition of nationhood, Ireland, through us, summons her children to her flag and strikes for her freedom.

Having organised and trained her manhood through her secret revolutionary organisation, the Irish Republican Brotherhood, and through her open military organisations, the Irish Volunteers and the Irish Citizen Army, having patiently perfected her discipline, having resolutely waited for the right moment to reveal itself, she now seizes that moment, and, supported by her exiled children in America and by gallant allies in Europe, but relying in the first on her own strength, she strikes in full confidence of victory.

We declare the right of the people of Ireland to the ownership of Ireland, and to the unfettered control of Irish destinies, to be sovereign and indefeasible. The long usurpation of that right by a foreign people and government has not extinguished the right, nor can it ever be extinguished except by the destruction of the Irish people. In every generation the Irish people have asserted their right to national freedom and sovereignty; six times during the past three hundred years they have asserted it in arms. Standing on that fundamental right and again asserting it in arms in the face of the world, we hereby proclaim the Irish Republic as a Sovereign Independent State, and we pledge our lives and the lives of our comrades-in-arms to the cause of its freedom, of its welfare, and of its exaltation among the nations.

The Irish Republic is entitled to, and hereby claims, the allegiance of every Irishman and Irishwoman. The Republic guarantees religious and civil liberty, equal rights and equal opportunities to all its citizens, and declares its resolve to pursue the happiness and prosperity of the whole nation and of all its parts, cherishing all the children of the nation equally, and oblivious of the differences carefully fostered by an alien government, which have divided a minority from the majority in the past.

Until our arms have brought the opportune moment for the establishment of a permanent National Government, representative of the whole people of Ireland and elected by the suffrages of all her men and women, the Provisional Government, hereby constituted, will administer the civil and military affairs of the Republic in trust for the people.

We place the cause of the Irish Republic under the protection of the Most High God, Whose blessing we invoke upon our arms, and we pray that no one who serves that cause will dishonour it by cowardice, inhumanity, or rapine. In this supreme hour the Irish nation must, by its valour and discipline and by the readiness of its children to sacrifice themselves for the common good, prove itself worthy of the august destiny to which it is called.

Signed on Behalf of the Provisional Government,

THOMAS J. CLARKE.

SEAN Mac DIARMADA,   THOMAS MacDONAGH,
P. H. PEARSE,   EAMONN CEANNT,
JAMES CONNOLLY   JOSEPH PLUNKETT.

Introduction

1916 AND ALL THAT

In a few short years Ireland will celebrate the hundredth anniversary of the 1916 Easter Rising. One of the most powerful elements – and legacies – of the 1916 Rising was the 1916 Proclamation. Its words – 'The Republic guarantees religious and civil liberty, equal rights and equal opportunities to all its citizens, and declares its resolve to pursue the happiness and prosperity of the whole nation and all of its parts, cherishing all of the children of the nation equally ...' – have resonated down through the decades.

But how relevant is a document drafted at the start of the twentieth century to Ireland in the twenty-first century? As we anticipate the 2016 centenary, it is timely to revisit the Proclamation and to ask the question: if we had to write it today, what would we proclaim? What would a 2016 Proclamation contain?

EASTER 2006

I stood outside the GPO on Easter Sunday 2006 alongside 100,000 others. Like many, I was there for the spectacle as well as for the historical significance of the occasion. Like others, I applauded politely when Capt. Tom Ryan of the 6th Infantry

Battalion read the Proclamation shortly after noon – as Pearse had read it ninety years previously (though to a somewhat smaller, considerably more sceptical crowd).

And I felt proud. Proud, despite the mixed consequences of the Rising and despite the arcane language of the Proclamation itself. I stood there outside the GPO and felt proud about the country we had become largely due to the pivotal role of the 1916 Easter Rising and the ambitions articulated in the Proclamation. It isn't often these days that one gets to feel patriotic, outside of sporting events. And yet it was patriotism that I, and no doubt others, felt that day – a sense of pride born out of seeing my country and my fellow citizens celebrating our past and looking forward optimistically to the future.

But 2006 seems a long time ago now, so much has changed. Not only has our economic situation deteriorated considerably, our confidence as a nation has been shaken. We face an extraordinary set of challenges as a nation – some shared with others and some unique to Ireland. Challenges that, surely, make the events of 1916 and the words of the Proclamation irrelevant as guides to the choices we face and must make? Or are they?

Easter 2016

Easter Sunday falls on 27 March in 2016, much earlier than Easter Sunday 1916, which fell on 23 April (with the Rising commencing on Easter Monday, 24 April). But it is not just the date that will be different. Ireland in 2016 will obviously be a very different country to Ireland in 1916. But not everything will have changed. Ireland will still be a small nation on the world stage, buffeted by international and global forces, though hopefully not by war. The Irish will continue to be defined by 'identity' as well as by geography, shaped by Ireland's diaspora. And we will probably continue to be an island that is politically divided, each part having a very different relationship with our island neighbour, although hopefully our island will still be at peace.

These similarities with the Ireland of 1916, as well as the forthcoming centenary, justify, in my opinion, revisiting the 1916 Proclamation and reassessing its relevance to the challenges we will face in 2016 and beyond. Therefore the aim of this book is to examine what still resonates in the original Proclamation with Ireland and the Irish almost a century later, and to explore what a 2016 Proclamation might contain to inspire and guide us in the decades ahead.

I should stress that the aim is not to debate the 1916 Rising, its validity or its legacy. These issues have been the subject of much analysis over the past ninety years and I don't propose to add to an already voluminous literature on the subject. I am not an historian and frankly I am more interested in the future than in the past, moved as I am by the legacy others have left us.

In these difficult times, *2016: A New Proclamation for a New Generation* seeks to reconnect our thinking about Ireland's future with the ideas and ideals of the 1916 Proclamation and the men who inspired it. It challenges us to reconsider our 'august destiny', and to rethink the meaning of Ireland's 'exaltation among the nations' in an ever-changing world.

Is the approaching centenary of the 1916 Easter Rising something we should celebrate or ignore? We asked this question in the 2016 Survey and the answer was clear: the overwhelming majority of Irish people surveyed – 81 percent – think it is something we should celebrate.[1] Fewer than one in five think it should be ignored.

While gender and social class differences were not reflected in the answer to this question, there was a noticeable split in the views of people of certain ages: those aged under forty-five are more inclined to celebrate the centenary; those aged over forty-five are less inclined to do so (although a majority still would celebrate it).

A Story for our Future

This book follows the structure of the original 1916 Proclamation, taking each paragraph or section as a cue for an assessment of the relevance of the original to Ireland, both for today and tomorrow. Though it comprises a little over 500 words, the Proclamation nevertheless manages to condense a great deal of history, politics and policies into its few short paragraphs. As such, examining its component claims provides a fruitful basis for reassessing Ireland in the twenty-first century, the challenges we face and the way forward.

But this is not a history book. Rather, I want to look ahead to 2016 and beyond, and to draw inspiration from a critical examination of the ideas and words in the 1916 Proclamation to explore Ireland's future – if you like, to tell a story for our future. I conclude by asking what should a 2016 Proclamation contain? Here I try to distil in my own words – not pretending to channel the 'soul of Ireland' – how I feel such a proclamation might be written for a modern, more cynical and also more powerful audience than that of 1916. I do so mindful that, as the centenary approaches, such a rethinking of the original Proclamation could invigorate and inspire others to play their part in shaping Ireland's destiny.

And I ask: what would you be prepared to sign? What are the principles and goals in your life and the life of the nation that you would be prepared to stand up for, even go out and die for?

Will you sign it?

1

The People of Ireland

*The Provisional Government of the Irish Republic
to the People of Ireland.*

HISTORY REPEATS ITSELF

The 1916 Proclamation was not the first to proclaim an Irish Republic or to announce the existence of a Provisional Government. Indeed, the authors of the 1916 Proclamation were consciously restating and paraphrasing the previous proclamations of the Fenian Rising in 1867, and the even earlier Proclamation of Independence by Robert Emmet in 1803. The latter was heavily influenced, in turn, by the 1798 Declaration of the United Irishmen.[1]

Nor did the nationalist and republican tradition in Ireland hold a monopoly over 'Provisional Governments'. At the height of the Home Rule crisis in 1914, for example, unionists in what eventually became Northern Ireland warned that a provisional government was ready to take over in the event of Home Rule coming into force. They drew strength from almost half a million signatories to the 'Solemn Pledge & Covenant' drawn up in 1912 in opposition to Home Rule.

Moreover, the idea of a provisional government was not

confined to Ireland. Throughout the nineteenth and twentieth centuries, different nations found themselves at one point or another subject to the rule of a provisional government, however tenuous. The term simply communicated that the newly formed body was meant to be a holding exercise, so to speak, not a permanent fixture. The members of the said government were (usually) not elected, nor had they put their proposals to the vote. That would supposedly come afterwards. Very often the legitimacy of any provisional government lay in what we might now call the realities on the ground. Where such realities made the emergence of an 'official government' from the provisional one inevitable (as, for example, in the case of the Belgian Revolution in 1830), then legitimacy was assured. But where realities worked against the newly formed provisional government (for example in Russia under Kerensky's Provisional Government in 1917) then legitimacy would quickly dissipate.

This brief historical digression simply illustrates one of the abiding problems that has confronted – and still confronts – governments everywhere: whence their legitimacy? The seven signatories of the 1916 Proclamation – Clarke, Mac Diarmada, MacDonagh, Pearse, Ceannt, Connolly and Plunkett – simply assumed their own legitimacy, as had the Fenians and Emmet before them. However, their behaviour was not unprecedented and it tapped into a very powerful vein of emotions and values relating to patriotism and national identity. To this day all governments rely on the same sense of belonging and shared identity to maintain their legitimacy. But is it enough anymore?

We the People

What makes a 'people'? This is not an easy question to answer. A people can be defined in terms of nationality, ethnicity, race, religion, language, history and geography, or some combination of these. Such matters of definition may have appeared straightforward to the signatories of the 1916 Proclamation. But the history of the twentieth century paints a far more complex, more nuanced picture. As Watson *et al.* remind us:

> According to many authors, a nation is formed as a result of people living together generation after generation, sharing a common territory, common economic life, common language and common physiological make-up, which are manifested in a common culture. Thus, a nation is a group of people with shared characteristics ...
>
> Added to this homogeneity and exclusivity is the demand contained in nationalist ideology that each nation should have self-determination; that it should have its own state. National identity is often characterised as having served to unite peoples in pursuit of statehood in the nineteenth and twentieth centuries ... In this case nationalism situates the source of individual identity within the people, who are perceived as the bearers of sovereignty and the basis of communal solidarity ... The point of relevance here is that although nation and state are not synonymous, they are often presumed or expected to be.[2]

And yet being Irish is as much an identity as a nationality. Irish people abroad – and their descendants – may live in other states, work and vote as well as paying their taxes there, but they often still consider themselves Irish. This was true in 1916 as it will be true in 2016: the Irish people are not the same as the people of Ireland. The Irish diaspora at the start of the twentieth century ensured a constant flow of communications, finances, people and ideas between the Irish in Ireland and the Irish elsewhere, and this situation continues today.

So as we approach 2016, what does it mean to be Irish? Watson *et al.* give us some clues, from studies that have tracked changing Irish attitudes in recent decades, specifically attitudinal surveys in 1995 and 2003.[3] They examined six separate dimensions that measure 'Irishness', three of them based on the idea of citizenship and three based on ethnicity, namely:

Citizenship
- to have been born in Ireland
- to have Irish citizenship
- to have lived in Ireland most of one's life
Ethnicity
- to be able to speak Irish
- to be a Catholic
- to feel Irish

Across all six dimensions there has been a decline in the percentages feeling that each is 'very important' for being Irish between 1995 and 2003. Nevertheless, the most recent figures show that Irish citizenship is still considered by the majority (59 percent) of Irish people to be a very important factor in being Irish – this category achieved the highest score for any of the six dimensions. This is followed by being born in Ireland (53 percent) and then by feeling Irish (50 percent).

Ireland is not alone in witnessing a fall in the importance of some of the six measures of national identity in recent years.[4] But Ireland is unique in certain regards when compared to other countries. For example, we have by far the lowest percentage of people agreeing that being able to speak one's national language, i.e. Irish, is very important (just 13 percent agreed in 2003). We also experienced the biggest fall in the percentage of people agreeing that 'feeling Irish' as part of their national identity is very important; to considerably lower levels indeed than two other English-speaking ex-colonies, namely Canada and New Zealand (in terms of 'feeling Canadian' or 'feeling like a New Zealander' respectively).

A Sense of Belonging

Nevertheless, research and trends only tell us *what* people believe makes a 'people'. But the more important question is *why* people want to belong to a nation or to an ethnic group. Richard English gets to the essence of nationalism and national identity thus:

> If we are to understand the appeal and power and nature of nationalism – to address the explanatory 'why?' of nationalism as well as the more descriptive 'what?' – then we need to consider the psychological processes which underlie it, and to grasp the emotional as well as the material rewards that it offers. Our physical needs (food, protection, the exchange of goods) cannot be met by acting singly, and our sense of meaning through identity again demands our belonging to a group – and ideally our belonging to one which we perceive to be special

... The essence of all this is the consensual loyalty which people give to a community, a community with which one can communicate in ways which in turn provide the foundations for meaningful lives, as we organise and interpret our knowledge of the surrounding world.[5]

English rightly stresses the emotional reality of nationalism:

Given this, the supposedly bizarre emotional attachment so commonly felt by people towards the symbols of their nation seems much less perplexing. Such intense sentiment emerges because people are thereby attached to a magnified, dignified version of themselves and their interests. If I am a nationalist, then my culture is special, distinctive and – despite the ubiquity of nations – unique; it bestows prestige upon my individual life; it enjoys my loyalty, and I will strive that it should receive both protection and also due recognition of its special value. All this relates nationalist community to the deepest human instincts, since the perceived specialness of each nation and each nationalism reflects the universal human desire for status, dignity, self-respect, pride and prestige ... Why does one become a nationalist? In part, because communal-national culture has so much to offer in response to the deepest human instincts.

We might describe and define national identity in terms of objective measures (such as birthplace), but the lived reality of being part of a people is a deeply emotional, subjective experience, and a perfectly valid one for all that, given its resonance with our most fundamental needs as human beings.

Mixed in with such feelings and experiences of national identity and nationalism is the concept of patriotism. They are not necessarily the same: indeed some Irish people describe themselves as 'patriots' but reject the label of 'nationalist'. Why is this? Eldad Davidov has studied this issue in European countries and makes an important distinction between blind and constructive patriotism.[6] 'Blind patriotism' is characterised as 'a rigid and inflexible attachment to country, characterised by unquestioning positive evaluation', while 'constructive patriotism' is described as 'an attachment to country characterised by critical loyalty'. As he notes, both orientations are indeed patriotic in the sense of having positive identifications with the nation. However, the blind patriot considers criticism of the state as disloyal, whereas constructive patriots may criticise the state if they feel that the state violates their ideology or if they believe the state is mistaken. Blind patriotism may manifest itself as a form of nationalism characterised by a love of the nation and state that is also distorted by negativity towards those not of the nation (and/or from other nations). Constructive patriotism on the other hand may manifest itself as a love of one's country and one's people without a necessarily close or affectionate relationship with the state and the nation as a political entity.

What then of the state of patriotism in Ireland today? As it happens, the Irish are one of the most patriotic nations on earth – if you take national pride as an indicator of patriotism. According to Smith and Kim:

> National identity is the cohesive force that both holds nation-states together and shapes their relationships with the family of nations. National pride is the positive effect that the public feels towards their country as a result of their national identity. It is both the pride or

sense of esteem that a person has for one's nation and the pride or self-esteem that a person derives from one's national identity.

National pride is related to feelings of patriotism and nationalism. Patriotism is love of one's country or dedicated allegiance to same, while nationalism is a strong national devotion that places one's own country above all others. National pride co-exists with patriotism and is a prerequisite of nationalism, but nationalism extends beyond national pride, and feeling national pride is not equivalent to being nationalistic.[7]

Their analyses of the International Social Survey Programme (ISSP) surveys on national identity in 1995–96 and again in 2003–04 show a very high level of patriotism in Ireland. In fact, measuring national pride across ten different domains (e.g. sporting prowess, history, arts, economic achievement) places Ireland third after Venezuela and the United States among all the countries sampled in the more recent survey (we were number 1 in the earlier survey).

So our strong sense of patriotism is relatively unique in the world. However, in other regards we are just like everywhere else: men are more patriotic than women (on average, in almost all countries) and older adults are more patriotic than younger adults (again on average, across all countries). But the fact that Ireland has such a high level of national pride *and* a relatively young population indicates just how deep such feelings are in Ireland.

One other interesting finding emerges from the ISSP surveys. It seems that English-speaking former colonies (specifically Canada, the United States, Australia, New Zealand and Ireland) score more highly in terms of national pride than either the United Kingdom or many other countries with predominantly European populations that were never colonised. Perhaps this is a result of having once been part of an empire.

In 1916 Ireland, Scotland, Wales and England were one nation-state. We shared the same language, legal system and currency. Nearly 100 years later are we still more-or-less the same 'people'? In the 2016 Survey we asked whether people agreed or disagreed that *These days there is little real difference between the Irish and the English?*

Precisely half of all Irish adults disagreed, 27 percent of them 'strongly', whilst over a third (36 percent) agreed, 12 percent of them 'strongly'. Disagreement was stronger amongst 16–24-year-olds, those living in Dublin and in higher social class groups.

eREPUBLIC

All these considerations of patriotism, nationalism and national pride refer to the singular concept of the nation or country. But can a concept that for the most part emerged in the nineteenth century, and provoked bloody conflict and division in the twentieth century, remain relevant to the evolving needs of the twenty-first century? After all, we live in an age of global economic forces, truly global networks of communications and the emergence of pan-national, political structures such as the European Union. Not to mention issues demanding a global response, such as climate change.

Yet there is some evidence that young people in Ireland are less enamoured with the EU than their older compatriots.[8] There is nothing inexorable, therefore, about the demise of either nationalist sentiment or the rise of post-nationalist values in countries such as Ireland. Indeed announcements about the death of the nation-state (like those of religion) have been premature so far. If anything, the Irish might be less immune to the nation's demise than in other countries given our dual identity as both a nationality *and* as an ethnic group (comprising some 70 million members worldwide depending on which definition you use).

The latter means that there is a global Irish community emotionally and financially engaged with Ireland's interests and prospects. A clear example of this was the Global Irish Economic Forum held in Farmleigh, Dublin, in September 2009.[9] In his opening address at the forum, Taoiseach Brian Cowen, TD, noted that:

> There is, of course, no exclusive definition of what it means to be Irish. Nor should there be. We are a country of just over 4 million people yet millions more around the world claim Irish descent. We are proud of our diaspora and view all those who have an affinity with our island as a great resource.
>
> Time and again, that resource has paid dividends in Ireland's past. In recent times, we have all seen how the global Irish played a critical role in the peace process in Northern Ireland, either as individuals or as members of flagship organisations, such as the Ireland Funds.
>
> It is entirely appropriate that one of the consequences of the Good Friday Agreement, which sets in train a new era of peace on

this island, was the insertion in Article 2 of the Irish Constitution of the statement that: *'the Irish nation cherishes its special affinity with people of Irish ancestry living abroad who share its cultural identity and heritage'* …

All of our global community has played – and must continue to play – an important role in the economic development of this island.

A return to emigration among Irish young people will once again reinforce connections between the 'Irish of Ireland' and the 'Irish of descent'. But the experience of emigration will be qualitatively different to that of previous generations. Facilities such as Facebook and Twitter – as well as mobile phones and Skype – now mean that there isn't the same emotional distance between emigrants and home, as there was in the past. Low cost airlines make it much cheaper to come back from time to time. In reality the digital tribes and communities we belong to are as important for some people, some of the time, as 'real' communities of geography, interest and occupation.

In the 2016 Survey we asked whether people agreed or disagreed that *Young people are better off staying in Ireland than moving abroad?*

Nearly half (47 percent) of all Irish people disagreed, 20 percent of them 'strongly', whilst a quarter agreed, 10 percent of them 'strongly'. Disagreement was strongest amongst 16–24-year-olds and women.

It isn't too difficult to imagine that the means might be found to enable suitably qualified emigrants to vote in Irish elections (e.g.: those who have left Ireland in the recent past). Such has been the demand of emigrants and their representatives for many decades. In the past, it has been rejected as unfeasible as well as potentially undemocratic.[10] But at least feasibility is becoming less of a problem these days in terms of secure, global communications.

> In the 2016 Survey, 40 percent of Irish people said they would like to see the right to vote in Irish elections given to Irish emigrants living abroad by 2020, though fewer than one in four expects it to happen by then.

In this scenario, Ireland might not so much merge into a post-national super-Europe as evolve into an eRepublic. Such a nation would be one that recognises the legitimate role of Irish emigrants in shaping their home country's future, as they live abroad earning money and building businesses that may ultimately benefit Ireland.

IRLANDIA

In mid 2009 there were just over 3.5 million adults in the Republic of Ireland (aged 15 and over), of whom 445,000 – or 12.6 percent of the adult population – were non-Irish nationals.[11] Five years previously non-Irish nationals numbered 247,000 or 7.7 percent of the adult population. Over two-thirds of this increase was due to migrants from the EU accession states, like Poland.

With over one in eight adults in Ireland not of Irish descent, what are the implications for Irishness and Irish identity? If recent immigrants follow the pattern of previous immigrants (and remember, there were no aboriginal peoples in Ireland – we're all descended from 'immigrants'), then many will most likely stay. But such an outcome is far from certain for the obvious reason that immigrants *to* Ireland are subject to many of the same forces as emigrants *from* Ireland described above: they retain deep emotional and communicative connections with their home countries simply because it is much easier and cheaper than ever before for them to do so. Indeed recently some limited data has suggested that many immigrants to Ireland are leaving due to the lack of employment opportunities.

Either way it is unlikely that Irish identity will be profoundly changed by immigration. This is not just because both the numbers and share of immigrants in the total population has peaked and already begun to decline, but also because they do not represent a sufficiently 'homogenous but different' group to challenge the dominant features of Irish identity. The Polish, for example, are the largest single group of recent immigrants and they are, for the main part, ethnically white and Catholic, just like the host population. In fact, the largest single group of non-Irish nationals are the English (just as in 1916). Again, they are too similar to the host population to create cultural cleavages that might challenge the dominant national identity. This is in marked contrast to many other EU member states which have experienced significant immigration in recent years, mostly comprising immigrants who were non-white and/or Muslim.

It seems that the people of Ireland in 2016 would be very recognisable to the people of 1916 as far as traditional images of the Irish and Irishness go.

REPUBLIC OF CHOICE

What is a republic? In common usage we understand it to mean government by representatives elected by some or all of the people. This is the norm for most of the European Union, though there are also a number of constitutional monarchies such as those in the United Kingdom, Sweden, Belgium, Denmark, Spain and the Netherlands. The word republic comes from the Latin *res publica* – usually translated as 'affairs of the people' or sometimes 'commonwealth'. It does not necessarily equate to democracy. There are numerous 'republics' around the world – and down through history – that are far removed from the liberal democratic ideal we take for granted in Ireland.

The 1916 Proclamation was not the first to proclaim a republic in Ireland. Robert Emmet solemnly declared in 1803 that 'our object is to establish a free and independent republic in Ireland'. This distinguished Emmet from the Society of United Irishmen, whose failed rebellion only five years previously, while seeking freedom from British rule, had not, in fact, demanded a republic, despite the influences of the American and French revolutions on Irish society's politics and ambitions.

It isn't even clear that the proclaimers of the Irish Republic in 1916 were entirely 'republican' in the political sense. At the time, republican in an Irish context was often used as a label for those advocating the use of violence to secure independence from Britain, rather than denoting a distinct philosophy about the ideal organisation of Irish political structures and society. Such confusion is reflected in some of the discussions among the rebels themselves in 1916, as Clair Wills notes:

> The rebels themselves, for the most part, understood their fight in terms of national self-determination. The principal issue was the takeover of political power. They were claiming the same rights for Ireland as for other European nations, conceived in the mould of nineteenth-century theories of national distinction rather than anti-colonial liberation. The idea of the Republic for the majority of the rebels meant not a radical social programme but national sovereignty.
>
> Indeed, for a great many of the Volunteers, republicanism meant simply physical force as opposed to constitutional means of gaining independence. It did not even necessarily imply a particular form of government. Inside the GPO, the rebels discussed the merits and demerits of inviting the German prince, Joachim, youngest son of Kaiser Wilhelm II, to become monarch, in the confident belief that within a few generations of intermarriage the Royal Family would become truly Irish.[12]

It took an independent Irish state twenty-seven years to eventually declare itself a Republic in 1949. Over sixty years later, it is unlikely that the people of Ireland would prefer any other arrangement – despite the continued conflation of 'Irish republicanism' with violent protest and dissent in the ensuing decades.

These days members of royal families are appreciated more for their celebrity lifestyles than for their leadership potential, so I don't expect any weakening of our attachment to republicanism by 2016, or a search for prospective royalty in need of adoption. But the roots of our republicanism are nevertheless quite shallow, not helped by our continuing inability to decide how best to govern ourselves, as explored in the next section.

> In the 2016 Survey, nearly two in five (37 percent) Irish people thought it likely that Britain's Queen Elizabeth would make her first visit to Ireland by 2020, and over a third (34 percent) said they would like her to visit, 31 percent would not like it and the balance were indifferent to the idea.

A Surfeit of Governance?

In his book, *The Best is Yet to Come*, Marc Coleman observes that Ireland has not one, but 'one hundred' governments:

From the mists of the nineteenth century, Ireland has inherited twenty-nine county councils, five county boroughs, five borough corporations, forty-nine urban district councils and twenty-six boards of town commissioners. Even the capital city is fragmented: instead of having one unified council, Dublin is managed by four separate local authorities …

As well as a national government, Ireland is also governed by regional governments (in theory), local government and a growing number of official but unaccountable organisations …

In 1994, eight regional authorities were established, authorities with shapes and sizes that, from a planning point of view, are strategically sensible. One of them – Dublin – was an amalgamation of the four local authority areas that filled its county border …

One central government with fifteen departments is joined by two aforementioned regional assemblies (there is a strong case for abolishing these), the eight aforementioned regional authorities, and over one hundred local authorities. Heading into the twenty-first century, we are relying on structures of local government invented over a hundred years ago.[13]

This is a long way from a single 'Provisional Government'. In addition to increasingly unwieldy (and unaffordable) local government structures, the British also left us the Single Transferable Vote system of Proportional Representation. De Valera modified the system slightly by insisting in the 1932 Constitution that only TDs thus elected could serve as ministers in the national government, with no scope to bring in others with experience and expertise to serve on the cabinet (as happens in several other countries, including the UK). As a result, as noted by Dan O'Brien:

The Irish electoral system is effectively unique and produces a unique political class. Positively, the politicians that emerge from it are plugged into their local communities. But it is also the main reason for the relatively low calibre of Irish elected representatives. Publicans, local solicitors, schoolteachers and the occasional GP simply do not have the expertise and experience to deal with the complexities of modern government in a highly internationalised setting. This is compounded by the absence of any incentive for those representatives to be agents of change. Politicians who live or die politically by addressing local concerns exclusively do not gain a jot by proposing healthcare reform, the adoption of best practice in public budgeting or the honing of diplomatic focus.[14]

The consequences of being over-governed by non-specialists are now plain for all to see.

THE PEOPLE OF EUROPE

A more positive feature of the Irish political system is the requirement to hold a referendum each time Ireland is required to agree to a new European Union treaty. The positive aspect is the opportunity it provides to the people of Ireland to debate to what extent they wish to be part of the people of Europe. A negative feature of such debates has been the extent to which our future in Europe is so rarely part of the actual 'debate', diverted as such referenda are by sometimes more local (and often irrelevant) issues.

The two Lisbon Referenda in 2008 and 2009 threw up one interesting trend. The percentage of Irish people opposed to Ireland's membership of the European Union actually increased between the referenda, even though the Yes vote rose as well.[15] However, the reality, as we approach the centenary of 1916, is that Ireland is now deeply integrated into the economic and political governance of the European Union via the euro currency and extensive treaties. Such a concept (the peaceful pooling of sovereignty by independent, democratic nations) was unimaginable to the authors of the 1916 Proclamation –

and not just because of the horrors of the First World War, then less than halfway towards its conclusion in November 1918. In 1916, Europe (and the rest of the world for that matter) was still coming to terms with the nature and necessity of nation-states. Indeed, the war's origins partially lay in the secessionist ambitions of countries and nationalist groups within both the Austro-Hungarian and Ottoman empires. The break up of other European empires further afield lay some decades ahead, but can likewise be traced back to the imperial tensions that preceded the First World War.

To generalise, the international momentum of nationalism in 1916 was very much away from pan-national political structures (voluntary or otherwise) and towards more independent, separatist nation-states (almost always achieved by violent conflict). This stands in marked contrast to the world we live in today. No more than those in 1916 could imagine a Europe at peace, can we imagine a Europe at war in 2016.

Europe now has a president (or permanent president of the European Council, from December 2009, to be precise: Herman van Rompuy until May 2012), again unimaginable in 1916. But this devolution of powers begs the question: who governs Ireland? Certainly not any one of the 'hundred governments' referred to earlier. And neither are we governed by the European Council, the European Commission nor the European Parliament. They do, however, all have some say in the governing of the Irish people.

The great European narrative for more than fifty years has been the gradual pooling of sovereignty, where appropriate, by the European Union's twenty-seven member states comprising some 500 million people. It is a voluntary pan-national political, social and economic structure, quite unlike anything attempted anywhere else before. Ireland has willingly partaken in this process and benefited significantly from doing so. The Irish have consistently been among the most 'pro-EU' of its member nations, despite the occasional No vote.

> In the 2016 Survey we asked whether people agreed or disagreed that *I think of myself as Irish first and European second?*
> Over three in four Irish people (78 percent) agreed, 63 percent of them 'strongly'. Agreement was strongest among 16–24-year-olds. Only one in ten disagreed.

By 2016, Ireland will have been a member of the EU for forty-three years (or the EEC as it was when we joined in 1973). But already a new chapter is beginning in Ireland's relationship with Europe, driven by the economic crisis (ours is one of the severest among eurozone countries) and by a 'mature reflection' on how we want that relationship to develop in future. Until now, political dialogue about Ireland in Europe has been characterised by a 'cosy consensus' that has shown little tolerance for dissenting views, perhaps as a consequence of the Social Partnership model, which has tended to value consensus above everything else. There was a certain degree of inevitability about this given the broadly 'win-lose' choices we faced in the past (especially as a net recipient of EU funding). It is difficult, however, to envisage a European agenda that will present such clear choices about the 'right thing to do' for Ireland in the future.

I expect more tensions between the people of Ireland and the people of Europe in the coming decades. The collective decisions that we will have to make in Europe in the years ahead may well be ones that are to the advantage of Europe in the long run, but to Ireland's disadvantage in the short run (e.g. bailouts to countries in economic difficulty that necessitate higher contributions from Irish taxpayers). Hopefully the future challenges we will face collectively in Europe will be resolved using the same soft powers that have helped Europe succeed over the past half century.[16]

IT'S OFFICIAL

By 2016, Ireland will have among the highest levels of personal debt per capita *and* government borrowings relative to GDP of any developed country in the world. The fallout from our long, debt-fuelled property boom that peaked in 2007 will still reverberate a decade later. The greater part of current and future government borrowings comprise 'IOUs' to foreign bond-holders, which have to be repaid – with interest – by Irish taxpayers. These bond-holders are a mixture of international pension funds (in the United States, China and elsewhere), central banks of other countries and the European Central Bank itself. They officially have a right to a large part of the future incomes and wealth generated in Ireland that must be collected in taxes to make the repayments.

Our capacity for self-governance as a nation – our Republic – will be severely constrained by the consequences of past profligacy. We are not alone in that regard (the federal constitutional republic that is the United States of America faces a similar dilemma in relation to its Chinese bond-holders). But it would be appropriate in the context of 2016 to reconsider our record of governing an Irish Republic on behalf of the Irish people, and to determine never again to let the greed and stupidity of a few endanger the freedom and well-being of the many.

IDEAS FOR THE 2016 PROCLAMATION

We still wish to be a Republic, and we still see ourselves as a distinct, Irish people. We know, nevertheless, that 'no nation is an island' and that our destiny is very much entwined with that of the rest of Europe.

Therefore our 2016 Proclamation must address a wider audience and recognise the limits of self-governance in the twenty-first century.

2

The Dead Generations

IRISHMEN AND IRISHWOMEN:
In the name of God and of the dead generations from which
she receives her old tradition of nationhood, Ireland, through
us, summons her children to her flag and strikes for her
freedom.

HOPE & HISTORY

History isn't history any more. At least not of the kind many Irish people grew up with. Throughout most of the twentieth century, history in Ireland seemed omnipresent – overbearing even. North of the border history kept on going, with each new wave of violent protest and dissent claiming direct lineage from the last wave, all the way back through history. South of the border, history encamped on the political landscape in the form of leading figures (de Valera, for example) and was embalmed in the Civil War parties that wrestled one another down through the decades.

And then it stopped. On Good Friday, 10 April 1998. Or so it seemed at the time. The agreement signed that day by the British and Irish governments, and by most of Northern Ireland's political parties, represented a new beginning. A few weeks later, on 23 May 1998, voters in separate referenda in

Northern Ireland and the Republic of Ireland ratified the key tenets of the agreement. Subsequently, on 2 December 1999, the constitutional and legal changes thus agreed came into effect. History, of a certain kind, had come to an end.

The crucial decision for voters in the south was whether to re-write Articles 2 and 3 of *Bunreacht na hÉireann* (the Constitution of Ireland), in force since December 1937. The original articles read as follows:

Article 2

The national territory consists of the whole island of Ireland, its islands and the territorial seas.

Article 3

Pending the re-integration of the national territory, and without prejudice to the right of the parliament and government established by this constitution to exercise jurisdiction over the whole territory, the laws enacted by the parliament shall have the like area and extent of application as the laws of Saorstát Éireann and the like extra-territorial effect.

The new Articles 2 and 3 are as follows:

Article 2

It is the entitlement and birthright of every person born in the island of Ireland, which includes its islands and seas, to be part of the Irish nation. That is also the entitlement of all persons otherwise qualified in accordance with law to be citizens of Ireland. Furthermore, the Irish nation cherishes its special affinity with people of Irish ancestry living abroad who share its cultural identity and heritage.

Article 3

1. It is the firm will of the Irish nation, in harmony and friendship, to unite all the people who share the territory of the island of Ireland, in all the diversity of their identities and traditions, recognising that a united Ireland shall be brought about only by peaceful means with the consent of a majority of the people, democratically expressed, in both jurisdictions in the island. Until then, the laws enacted by the Parliament established by this Constitution shall have the like area and extent of application as the laws enacted by the Parliament that existed immediately before the coming into operation of this Constitution.

2. Institutions with executive powers and functions that are shared between those jurisdictions may be established by their respective responsible authorities for stated purposes and may exercise powers and functions in respect of all or any part of the island.

These amendments represented the culmination of a long, drawn-out process of clarifying precisely who the 1916 Proclamation was addressing as 'Irishmen and Irishwomen'. The unionists of Northern Ireland, from the signatories of the Ulster Covenant onwards, had no desire to be governed from Dublin as a minority on the island. The advent of partition solved this problem for unionists, but in doing so created another reluctant minority – this time comprising nationalists living in Northern Ireland. The Good Friday Agreement was an attempt – over eighty years later – to reconcile these overlapping dualities of majority/minority relations on the island of Ireland.

THE DEAD DON'T VOTE

Growing up a nationalist in Northern Ireland during the 1960s and 1970s left me in no doubt about the wishes of 'the dead generations'. Then, as before, nationalists saw the creation of Northern Ireland as an unwarranted compromise; a short term solution that was unsustainable in the long term. The authors of the 1916 Proclamation no doubt hoped that unionists – to the extent they were given much thought – would see reason and side with the tide of history, in the spirit say, of Wolfe Tone and the other Protestant leaders of the United Irishmen at the end of the eighteenth century. By the 1970s, however, reason was replaced by force as the preferred solution to unionist intransigence (as well as in response to their repression of nationalists).

At times of turmoil and rapid change, history can weigh heavily on the minds of those affected. Many draw succour from history as a source of continuity and, for that matter, of certainty. Even as late as the 1970s, I recall that the result of the 1918 general election – the last island-wide vote, which saw Sinn Féin candidates elected to the Westminster parliament in 73 out of 103 Irish constituencies – was used by some nationalists to argue that Northern Ireland was democratically illegitimate. By then of course, most of the voting men and women (the latter aged over thirty, voting for the very first time) of 1918 were dead. They had joined the dead generations.

Writing at the time of the ninetieth anniversary of the 1916 Rising, Garret FitzGerald recognised the propensity of some to claim inherited legitimacy for their actions with reference to 1916 and its consequences:

> Clearly, there is much hindsight involved in what passes for today's conventional wisdom that condemns 1916 as 'undemocratic'. Many who now hold that view have been hugely influenced by a belief that the roots of the IRA violence in Northern Ireland are to be found in 1916.
>
> It is true that the IRA and Sinn Féin have sought to use 1916 as an excuse or cover for their violence against the unionist community in Northern Ireland, and far too many people have allowed them to get away with that tactic. But the truth is that neither the often sectarian motivation of the IRA in Northern Ireland nor the ruthlessness of their campaign against its unionist community find any parallel whatever in the 1916 Rising. It is not difficult to imagine the horror with which the 1916 leaders would have greeted today's attempts by the IRA to justify their past actions by reference to what happened in Dublin ninety years ago.[1]

No doubt the centenary of the Easter Rising in 2016 will induce yet more reflection, debate and argument about the legitimacy of the Rising and its consequences. The dead generations will still exert their influence from their graves, even on those who most vehemently reject their legacy.

New Traditions

Yet we still feel some connection, some indebtedness to the past. All peoples do: hence the prevalence of war memorials, remembrance days and so on. From whom does Ireland receive 'her old tradition of nationhood' in the twenty-first century? Or should that be *traditions*?

The 1916 Rising was preceded by a surge of interest in Irish culture, from the establishment of the Gaelic Athletic Association in 1884, to the founding of Conradh na Gaeilge in 1893. This resurgence was partly seen by many behind these and similar organisations as providing a corrective antidote to what was perceived as the ongoing – inexorable even – Anglicisation of Ireland. Their ethos was therefore both exclusionary and steeped in a particular view of Irish history and culture.

Today in Ireland we still have the GAA, but we also have access to a world of culture via the internet, satellite TV, and through the experience of foreign travel by the majority of Irish citizens. Not only do we have access to, but we are immersed in the cultures of other countries (especially English-speaking countries), as well as being more conscious of the other cultures present on the island of Ireland, be they speakers of Ulster-Scots or, for that matter, Polish.

And yet, as we saw in the previous chapter, Irish people are very proud of their country when compared with others. We are also proud of our culture: we take great pride in the success of Irish artists, performers, writers and musicians on the international stage. Of the ten Irish recipients of Nobel Prizes, for example, four have been for literature (five won the Nobel Prize for Peace, and one shared the Nobel Prize for Physics).[2] Culture is both the expression of various traditions as well as their creative reinterpretation by each new generation of inheritors. The success of *gaelscoileanna* over the past thirty years is just one example of the desire of living generations to maintain and reinvigorate one of the traditions of nationhood in Ireland. Some 38,000 children receive their education through the medium of Irish in 139 primary schools and 37 secondary schools throughout the island of Ireland (excluding schools in the Gaeltacht).[3]

In the 2016 Survey, only one in ten Irish adults think it likely there will be a resurgence of the Irish language by 2020. However, over two in five (44 percent) Irish people would like to see a resurgence, while 27 percent would not like it. The rest are indifferent.

Nevertheless, concepts of nationhood and national identity are much more pliable than in the past. We receive our tradition of nationhood and much else besides from many different sources. But perhaps most crucially, unlike those who drafted the 1916 Proclamation, our tradition of nationhood in the twenty-first century includes the history of having governed ourselves as a nation for nearly 100 years. Nationhood is no longer an 'old tradition' to be invoked in the absence of the real thing, rather it is a lived reality for millions of Irish men and women.

SECULAR CATHOLICS

In the 1911 Census preceding the 1916 Rising, there were 2.8 million Catholics in the twenty-six counties – comprising 90 percent of the population. In the 2006 Census, there were

3.7 million Catholics in the Republic of Ireland – some 88 percent of the population.[4] As in 1911, the Church of Ireland remained the second largest religious group in 2006 (though their numbers were significantly down from the 1911 figure).

Ireland in 2016 will therefore be a predominantly Catholic country, just as in 1916. However, exhortations in the name of God will mean different things to different people. For example, in marked contrast to 1911, Muslims rather than Presbyterians now make up the third largest religious group in Ireland: the 2006 Census counted nearly 33,000 followers of Islam (an increase of 70 percent on their numbers in the 2002 Census).

Ireland's constitution invokes God much as the 1916 Proclamation did, though in a more explicitly Christian manner. This from the preamble to *Bunreacht na hÉireann*:

> In the Name of the Most Holy Trinity, from Whom is all authority and to Whom, as our final end, all actions both of men and States must be referred,
>
> We, the people of Éire,
>
> Humbly acknowledging all our obligations to our Divine Lord, Jesus Christ, Who sustained our fathers through centuries of trial,
>
> Gratefully remembering their heroic and unremitting struggle to regain the rightful independence of our Nation,
>
> And seeking to promote the common good, with due observance of Prudence, Justice and Charity, so that the dignity and freedom of the individual may be assured, true social order attained, the unity of our country restored, and concord established with other nations,
>
> Do hereby adopt, enact, and give to ourselves this Constitution.

The special status afforded the Catholic church in Ireland both before and after Irish independence has ebbed significantly in the past decade, accelerated by the seemingly endless litany of scandals concerning child sex abuse by clergy and subsequent cover ups. In 2009, the Murphy Report, following a commission of investigation into the handling of allegations of child abuse against clerics of the Catholic Archdiocese of Dublin by church and state authorities, represented an historic rupture in church-state relations in Ireland. As the historian Ronan Fanning observed:

> Partition created an unnaturally large Catholic majority in the 26 counties by amputating the Protestants of north-east Ulster who might otherwise have ameliorated the overweening Catholic triumphalism that came to characterise the Irish Free State ...
>
> The impact of the Civil War was less obvious but arguably more insidious. Church and state shared a common concern to forge a national identity in the post-war aftermath of shame and disappointment ...
>
> The paramount reason why the Murphy report is such an historic landmark is because of the historic responses its avoidance of equivocation has elicited across the political spectrum ...
>
> The most immediate and impressive reaction in Fianna Fáil came from Minister for Justice Dermot Ahern: 'This is a republic – the people are sovereign – and no institution, no agency, no church can be immune from that fact' ...
>
> The wheel of church-state relations has indeed begun to turn full circle when politicians are now competing in their expressions of anti-Vatican sentiments where in previous decades they competed in burnishing their Catholic credentials; that, in Pat Rabbitte's words,

the Vatican seems 'to misunderstand the earthquake they have set off in Irish society. Whatever happens, it is the end of the age of deference.'[5]

Earlier rumblings in the earthquake that befell church-state relations in Ireland could be witnessed during the 1980s and 1990s, for example with the legalisation of the sale of condoms without prescription in 1985 and the referendum legalising divorce in 1995. A new framework for church-state relations in the Republic of Ireland is being forged in light of the fallout from the Murphy Report and subsequent revelations. The accusation in 1912–14 by Unionist opponents that 'Home Rule is Rome Rule' was subsequently borne out by much of what happened after partition. Indeed, partition effectively made a culture of 'Rome Rule' almost inevitable in the Republic of Ireland. Such an accusation will not apply as readily to Ireland in 2016.

However, despite the irreversible changes to church-state relations in Ireland, the Irish themselves remain among the most religiously observant people in Europe. According to the World Values Survey in 1999–2000 (the most recent available comparative data), Ireland has the second highest incidence of church-going in Europe (75 percent going once a week or more often) after Malta (86 percent).[6] Moreover, there is some evidence that church-going is on the increase in Ireland, perhaps as a result of the recession, as reported in a survey by the Iona Institute in October 2009.[7] It found that:

- 46 percent of adults aged over 18 attend church every week (up

> from 42 percent in an ESRI survey in late 2007/early 2008; though still far below the 79 percent in a similar survey in 1988–89).
>
> • The percentage not going every week but at least once a month stands at 19 percent, giving a total of 65 percent of adults attending church on a regular basis in Ireland.
> • 31 percent of 18–24-year-olds attend church weekly, a further 22 percent attend monthly.
> • 56 percent of those living in rural areas attend weekly, falling to 38 percent in Dublin.

Still there can be no doubt that the Irish have experienced a similar trend towards secularism and 'à la carte Catholicism' evident in other predominantly Catholic countries. One obvious indicator is the collapse of the practice among Catholics of going to confession. A 2007 survey by Dr Micheál MacGréil (with the ESRI and NUI Maynooth) found that 27 percent of Catholics go to confession 'several times a year or more frequently', whilst one-third have given up the practice altogether.[8] This contrasts with an equivalent figure of 80 percent going to confession in 1988–89 – indicating a drop of 53 percentage points in nineteen years.

In several respects, Ireland is moving to an arrangement that I would call 'secular Catholicism'. In other words, the vast majority of the population are self-described Catholics – happy to participate in key church-based celebrations such as baptisms, first holy communion, weddings, etc. – but otherwise quite secular in their values, lifestyle and outlook. One such indicator of the secular lifestyles of the Irish is the rise in the percentage of births outside marriage: from a low of 2 percent in 1960 to 32.4 percent in the first quarter of 2009.[9] Ireland is broadly in line with the EU average in this regard – somewhat ahead of other predominantly Catholic countries such as Poland and Italy, but behind France (though a long way from Greece at 6.5 percent of all births and Iceland at 64.1 percent in 2008).[10]

In most respects, this is not particularly surprising. When it comes to religious beliefs, the reality in the twenty-first century is that Ireland shares most of the characteristics of other developed countries. Those more likely to consider themselves to be religious in any given population tend to be women more than men, older people rather than younger people, and those whose formal education ended at primary or secondary levels.

A 2008 report by the US-based Pew Research Center plotted Gross Domestic Product (GDP) per capita against the percentage of the population in each country who agreed that 'religion is very important or somewhat important' in their lives. It showed a strong negative correlation of -0.8: in effect a straight-line relationship between economics and religiosity. The higher GDP per capita, the lower the reported level of belief.[11] Ireland was not included in the survey, but I know from asking the same question of Irish respondents in other surveys that Ireland is firmly in the same place on the chart as Britain, Australia and most of western Europe. The exception to this apparent economic determinism is the United States.

> In the 2016 Survey, the majority (56 percent) of Irish people said they would not like to see a referendum to remove all references to Christian beliefs from the Irish Constitution by 2020, and only one in five would welcome this. However, just 14 percent thought it likely that there would be such a referendum in that time frame.

Nevertheless, what seems to be happening in Ireland is that we are becoming what they call in Britain 'four-wheel Christians': we only come to church to be baptised in a pram, married in a limo and buried in a hearse!

Irish Exceptionalism

But just as we have American exceptionalism in matters religious, so also have we Irish exceptionalism. Indeed, it would be wrong to simply pigeonhole Ireland as 'just like everywhere else' when it comes to our experiences of Christianity and secularism. And as an economist I know better than to base analyses on naive economic determinism. It is rarely that simple. In fact, several aspects of our society's history and development add a unique perspective to the debate. Two in particular strike me:

1. The role of the Catholic Church in Ireland and its relatively recent, if meteoric, demise as a religious force.
2. The sectarian conflict in Northern Ireland and its continuation right up to the dawn of the twenty-first century.

In *Preventing the Future: Why was Ireland so poor for so long?* Tom Garvin reminds us of the extraordinary power the Catholic Church wielded in Ireland up to as recently as the 1990s.[12] Referring to the findings of various attitudinal surveys in the 1950s and 1960s, Garvin observes:

> It must be remembered that Irish religious culture was one of literal belief in God, Christ, the Virgin birth, miracles, saints, heaven, hell, purgatory, limbo and all the rest of it – a belief system partly pre-Christian in origin and certainly non-Christian in psychological texture.[13]

Garvin then describes the onset of secularisation in Ireland from the 1960s and 1970s right up to the present day, going on to note that:

> … the counter-example of the United States, a very religious country, indicates that the death of faith has nothing in particular to do with modernisation or economic development, but everything to do with politics. In particular, faith in the modern world seems to be liable to be poisoned by an overly intimate relationship between church and state, and, more generally, by an intimate relationship between ecclesiastical organisations and political power … In other words, Ireland is not so much becoming secularised … Rather, it is that Ireland is becoming declericalised.[14]

Ireland's exceptionally intimate relationship with the Catholic Church from cultural to social through to political levels is now rapidly giving way to something else. I suspect it will be something that does not fit neatly into two-dimensional models of economic development and secularisation.

But before exploring what that something else might be, let's look at the second aspect of Irish exceptionalism – Northern Ireland. Northern Ireland is by far the most religiously observant region of the UK – with 81 percent of the population describing themselves as Christian (versus a UK average of 53 percent) and 45 percent saying they attend church at least once a month (versus a UK average of 15 percent).[15]

Northern Ireland is going through its own rapid secularisation at present, brought on by the cessation of armed conflict between republican, loyalist and state forces. That cessation means that the traditional badges of religious identity and 'tribal' affiliation no longer need to be worn so explicitly as they were until quite recently. It may also lead to a more reflective approach to religious faith and practice, driven more by personal than by political imperatives.

The question, of course, is whether the normalisation of religious practices in Northern Ireland will affect the Republic. I suspect it will: if only because the traditional schism between Catholics and Protestants will lose its resonance with the younger generation now growing up on both sides of the border – leading to a more open and perhaps more experimental approach to religious insight and faith. As the saying goes, the young 'won't carry the limp' as their forefathers did before them. Moreover, we may see a less dualistic attitude towards political and religious relations on this island, one that still too readily defaults into a unionist/Protestant versus nationalist/Catholic mindset.

PROPELLING THE FUTURE

Where next then for Christianity in Ireland? Its future course will undoubtedly be shaped by global trends now underway, both at the level of ideas – for example, the challenge of the New Atheism – and at the level of institutions, in particular the European Union, seen from Ireland's perspective.

Anticipating the possible future direction of Christianity in Ireland does demand that we have a clear understanding of the role and impact of Christianity at a societal as well as at a personal level. In their book *Suicide of the West*, authors Richard Koch and Chris Smith note the pivotal role played by Christianity in shaping western civilisation – from Europe to America to Australasia.[16] All that we hold dear as westerners – democracy, freedom and equality between all human beings regardless of class, colour or gender – have their origins in Christianity's fusion of ancient Greek and Judaic teachings with its unique emphasis on individual integrity, agency and responsibility. Moreover, the free market economy is a uniquely western invention, which only became possible because of innovations such as those of Pope Gregory VII in the eleventh century, which created private property rights that could not be violated by monarchs or by the state. As Indian-born economist Deepak Lal has pointed out, only Christianity ended the despotism and poverty that typically prevailed under almost all other religious traditions.[17] The result is that some ten centuries later we have globalisation and a standard of living enjoyed by billions of people only available to the ruling class throughout most of human history.

In Ireland, we still enjoy the social capital built up through centuries of Christian faith and practices. The special emphasis on family life in Irish society is a crucially important legacy of our Christian past, and one reason for the relatively low incidence of divorce and family breakdown – so far. Christian tolerance and compassion has undoubtedly played a part in our country's remarkably trouble-free adjustment to immigration and with it the arrival of nearly half a million people of many different faiths and from many different countries in the past decade and more. Even some of our institutions – such as Social Partnership and the Seanad – have their origins in earlier Catholic social teachings such as vocationalism and corporatism.

Like all capital, our Christian social capital in Ireland can quickly be depleted unless preserved and reinvested. That in turn requires a far more public debate about our values than heretofore: not just in terms of what Americans call 'culture war' – issues such as abortion and gay marriage – but also about that quintessentially Christian question, i.e. what sort of life should we lead? And what sort of society is best suited to support the choice of a way of life?

We can see some hints of a debate about this question, for example, in relation to the emerging area of happiness research and the role of social, economic and psychological factors in enhancing or diminishing happiness. I suspect that the rich seam of Christian teachings on the good life, that build in turn on pre-Christian philosophies, has much to contribute here.

Likewise, Christians should see the popular distinction between 'spirituality' and 'religion' as an invitation to contribute to a more reflective, personal evaluation of how best to live in this world. After all, the distinction has a powerful heritage in Christianity's history – all the way back to Spinoza, one of the Enlightenment's greatest philosophers (who also happened to be Jewish).

Despite the shock to church-state relations from the Murphy Report and numerous other findings, it is highly unlikely that we will see the emergence of political hostility towards the Catholic church in Ireland such as the anti-clericalism evident throughout the nineteenth and twentieth centuries in countries such as Spain, Italy, France and Poland. Moreover, Ireland is becoming a more middle-aged society, accompanied by a baby boom, with the result that the Catholic church might loom larger in the lives of a growing number of Irish people (weddings, baptisms, schooling) than at any time in the past twenty years when we were 'the young Europeans'.[18]

Still the preservation of Irish Christian social capital demands a political response. The outpouring of anger following the Murphy Report illustrates the scale of the challenge. Someone once said that religion is spread through stories – not through theology, dogma or philosophy. It is the stories we tell one another, that we tell our children and that we tell the world about ourselves which provide the narrative for our individual and collective lives. So what stories will we tell about Ireland – about where we have come from and where we are going?

In 2016 the stories that will resonate most, and be the most effective, will be those that weave Christian values into the narrative. Thus, it will be possible to invoke the name of God in 2016 and most will still recognise God as a Christian God, though such invocations will increasingly be a matter of private preferences rather than the public pronouncements of Irish politicians.

Free to Fail

There are different kinds of freedom. There is political freedom – the kind the rebels of 1916 were prepared to fight for; personal freedom – the kind demanded by our increasingly secular society; and economic freedom – the kind with which we have had a more ambiguous relationship in Ireland. For much of Ireland's history as an independent country, we enjoyed political freedom without economic freedom. Not only was our economic freedom afflicted by an overdependence on the British market (tied, as we were, to a monetary union with sterling), but also our potential for economic freedom was curtailed domestically by state intervention and, worst of all, cronyism.

The excesses of the Celtic Tiger era in Ireland and the subsequent economic collapse illustrates the difficulties we have had securing our economic freedom. Ireland has too often let vested interests shape the direction of economic policy to the extreme detriment of the country and its citizens. John Kay made a similar point about the global crisis in his 2009 Wincott Lecture:

I am going to argue that there are three elements to the triumph of the market economy. The first I will describe under the heading of 'prices as signals': the price mechanism is generally a better guide to resource allocation than central planning. The second element is 'markets as a process of discovery': a chaotic process of experimentation is the means through which a market economy adapts to change. The third heading is 'diffusion of political and economic power'. The economic point here is that prosperity and growth require that entrepreneurial energy should be focused on the creation of wealth, rather than the appropriation of the wealth of other people.

In what we teach, in what we say, in our economic research and most importantly in the policies we adopt – we put too much emphasis on the first of these elements – prices as signals to guide resource allocation – at the expense of the, possibly more important, second and third elements – markets as process of discovery, markets as mechanism for the diffusion of political and economic power.

The result is that both supporters and critics of the market economy have often confused policies that are pro-business with policies that are pro-market. That confusion has both undermined the social and political legitimacy of the market economy, and led to serious policy errors that follow from a mistaken, or at least incomplete, understanding of how a market economy works.[19]

In Ireland, too many successive governments have adopted 'pro-business policies' over the years (favouring specific sectors – such as construction – rather than promoting broad, pro-market policies) that simply propped up current incumbents to the detriment of potential new entrants (and to the detriment of consumers in the affected markets). Ireland has rarely had explicitly 'free market' political parties (with the possible exception of the former Progressive Democrats in their early years). Too often, we have believed in the power of politicians and their appointees to 'second guess' the needs of the people rather than letting the markets figure such things out for themselves. Of course, Ireland has hardly been unique in this regard, nor were the 1916 rebels and their successors unique in imagining that a state-led path to economic development would lead to rising standards of living for everyone. Such notions were extremely popular at the time, long before it became clear just how difficult it was (and is) for the state and its managers to second-guess the needs of the wider population they earnestly hope to serve. It comes down to uncertainty. As John Kay observes:

> The world is uncertain: not just risky, but uncertain, in the sense used by Keynes and Knight. Not only do we not know which future outcomes will happen: we are unable to specify at all fully what these possible outcomes will be. If we could predict or anticipate the invention of the wheel, we would have already invented it. Market economies do not predict the future, they explore it. That is a fundamental – perhaps the fundamental – difference between a planned and a market economy.

But despite our economic failings since the foundation of the state, and more especially because of our economic successes, we Irish live in the most economically free country in Europe and the third freest in the world according to the Heritage Foundation's *Index of Economic Freedom 2009*.[20] The foundation defines economic freedom thus:

The highest form of economic freedom provides an absolute right of property ownership, fully realised freedoms of movement for labour, capital and goods, and an absolute absence of coercion or constraint of economic liberty beyond the extent necessary for citizens to protect and maintain liberty itself. In other words, individuals are free to work, produce, consume and invest in any way they please, and that freedom is both protected by the state and unconstrained by the state.

They measure scores under ten headings (business freedom, trade freedom, fiscal freedom, government size, monetary freedom, investment freedom, financial freedom, property rights, freedom from corruption, labour freedom) and then calculate the (unweighted) average to generate the overall freedom index score.

Of course, an obvious criticism of the *Index of Economic Freedom* is that it only addresses economic freedom – so freedom of the press, personal freedom etc., do not figure in their calculations. In fact, the complete list of 157 countries for which indices are produced shows a strong correlation between liberal democracy and economic freedom (not to mention standard of living). Indeed, the benefits of greater economic liberty include:

- Higher personal income
- Less unemployment
- Faster economic growth
- More macroeconomic stability
- Greater capital investment and productivity

- More business start-ups
- More entrepreneurship and innovation
- A better-educated workforce
- Less poverty and inequality
- Better health
- Greater population inflows
- A cleaner environment
- A better quality of life
- More democracy and peace

That is quite a list. All the more reason to defend and expand the freedoms we enjoy. After all, that is why we became a Republic in the first place. The *Economic Freedom of the World 2009 Report* showed that Ireland became economically freer between 2006 and 2007.[21] In fact we moved upwards in the international rankings: from number ten in 2006 to number seven in 2007 – the latest year for which sufficient comparative data is available for all the countries surveyed. Our neighbours across the water fell from number five to nine in the same period. The publishers of the Economic Freedom of the World (EFW) analyses – the Fraser Institute – defines economic freedom as comprising four components:

- personal choice
- voluntary exchange coordinated by markets
- freedom to enter and compete in markets
- protection of persons and their property from aggression by others

As they note:

Put simply, institutions and policies are consistent with economic freedom when they provide an infrastructure for voluntary exchange and protect individuals and their property from aggressors. In order to achieve a high EFW rating, a country must provide secure protection of privately owned property, even-handed enforcement of contracts, and a stable monetary environment. It also must keep taxes low, refrain from creating barriers to both domestic and international trade, and rely more fully on markets rather than the political process to allocate goods and resources.

Still, the muted Irish response to our success in these and other such rankings makes me feel that we wear our freedom lightly in Ireland. Worse, many of the measures used to generate the EFW rankings – government debt and bank independence for example – will be adversely affected by NAMA. It would be a tragedy if our hard-won economic freedom is one of the victims of the global recession of 2008–2010.

Of course, economic freedom was not a priority for the 1916 signatories. It seems unlikely that they gave much thought to taxation, trade and regulation, even though their world had recently experienced a period of extraordinary trade-led, global economic development, brought to an abrupt end by the Great War. Historian Niall Ferguson describes the period leading up to the Great War, which commenced just twenty-one months before the Easter Rising:

From around 1870 until World War I, the world economy thrived in ways that look familiar today. The mobility of commodities, capital and labour reached record levels; the sea-lanes and telegraphs across the Atlantic had never been busier, as capital and migrants travelled west and raw materials and manufactures travelled east. In relation to output, exports of both merchandise and capital reached volumes not seen again until the 1980s. Total emigration from Europe between 1880 and 1910 was in excess of 25 million. People spoke euphorically of 'the annihilation of distance'.[22]

Perhaps inevitably, much of the improvement in the material well-being of many of the world's citizens before the First World War that Ferguson describes, was taken for granted, much as we take such things for granted in our own time. The 1916 rebels were anything but advocates of free markets and laissez-faire economic policies (much more my own proclivity as an economist and businessman). Indeed, they would often lambast the perceived materialism of the British, seen in marked contrast to the spiritual superiority of the Irish (though how much the latter was simply compensating for failure to achieve much by way of the former is debatable).

Nevertheless, thanks to the efforts of both dead and living generations we enjoy a higher standard of living in Ireland, and comparatively greater wealth, that affords us considerably more freedom – political, personal and economic – than we have ever had before. Indeed, we have an expanding set of choices available to us, because of the choices made by our predecessors. The future will also be the outcome of the many choices freely made by individuals, businesses, policy-makers and communities today and tomorrow. For that we should be grateful, since that is how we got here in the first place and Ireland, in entering the second decade of the twenty-first century, is still a much, much better country than it was twenty, fifty or a hundred years ago. And it will be even better in 2016 because of that freedom.

As we approach 2016, we will be living in a world immensely more integrated than could have been imagined in 1916. It will also be a world characterised by considerable uncertainty and instability. Irish people will be free, within obvious constraints, to pursue opportunities also unimaginable in 1916. But freedom can be scary for some, as it entails making choices that have unforeseen consequences and being responsible for those consequences. Such was the reality facing the signatories of the 1916 Proclamation as they struck for freedom.

IDEAS FOR THE 2016 PROCLAMATION

The destinies of both parts of the island of Ireland are now bound together in mutual recognition of the freedoms of aspiration and choice available to all, including the importance of economic freedom to deliver future well-being. The Irish on both sides of the border will remain religious even as the church-state relationship evolves to a more secular one.

Therefore our Proclamation must recognise the historic settlement on the island of Ireland and the continuing importance of freedom to the lives of all.

3

Now Seizes That Moment

Having organised and trained her manhood through her secret revolutionary organisation, the Irish Republican Brotherhood, and through her open military organisations, the Irish Volunteers and the Irish Citizen Army, having patiently perfected her discipline, having resolutely waited for the right moment to reveal itself, she now seizes that moment, and, supported by her exiled children in America and by gallant allies in Europe, but relying in the first on her own strength, she strikes in full confidence of victory.

A Nation of Belongers

The Irish are a nation of belongers – we like to join things. It has been that way for a long time. In 1914, at the outbreak of the First World War, the Ulster Volunteer Force had some 100,000 members and the Irish Volunteers had nearly 200,000 members.[1] The Irish Citizen Army was a much smaller force of some 220 members; the secretive Irish Republican Brotherhood, by definition, had even fewer members (and were busy running the Irish Volunteers).

Fast forward to 2006 and a survey on volunteering by the Central Statistics Office. Although it was the height of the Celtic Tiger boom, when some felt that we were fixated on materialism to the detriment of our spirit, the survey found that:

- Almost two-thirds (65 percent) of persons aged 16 and over participated in at least one group activity.
- Overall, nearly one-quarter (24 percent) of people participated in informal, unpaid charitable work.
- Over half of the population aged 15 and over (52 percent) had at least six people they could turn to in times of need, while only 2 percent stated that they had nobody to ask for help.
- When asked, 85 percent of the people reported that they believed that by working together, people in their neighbourhood could influence decisions that affected them.[2]

Sports bodies are the main beneficiaries of our joining propensities these days. The GAA in particular benefits, with over 2,500 clubs throughout the island of Ireland. Apart from sport, there are other associations to join and participate in, such as trade unions (over 500,000 members or 31 percent of all employees in 2007).[3] In contrast to 1914, political organisations attract the least interest in twenty-first-century Ireland – only 1 percent of adults are actively involved in politics compared with 11 percent involved in sports-related activities.

E Pluribus Unum?

Emigration has been a recurring theme throughout Irish history, hence the Proclamation's reference to 'her exiled children'. More recently, Ireland has experienced an unprecedented level of immigration, with profound implications for our future, as well as for our sense of 'belonging'. The American sociologist Robert Putnam has examined the impact of immigration on host societies (in the United States, Canada, Holland and other countries). His conclusions are challenging:

> It would be unfortunate if a politically correct progressivism were to deny the reality of the challenge to social solidarity posed by diversity. It would be equally unfortunate if an historical and ethnocentric conservatism were to deny that addressing that challenge is both feasible and desirable. Max Weber instructed would-be political leaders nearly a century ago that 'politics is a slow boring of hard boards'. The task of becoming comfortable with diversity will not be easy or quick, but it will be speeded by our collective efforts and in the end well worth the effort.[4]

Putnam's paper is entitled 'E Pluribus Unum' – 'one out of many'. The motto has historically been that of the United States government, referring initially to the unity of the different states that came together after the war of independence and subsequently to the 'melting pot' ethnic mix of America after their civil war. The European Union has a similar motto, adopted in 2000: 'United in Diversity'.

The bottom line for Putnam is that immigration tends to undermine the 'social glue' that binds communities together (people are less trusting, watch more TV by themselves etc., when they experience rapid immigration). He acknowledges the point made by others that the benefits of immigration are evident at a national level (productivity, economic growth, labour supply etc.) but the costs are experienced by local communities (pressures on housing, education, health etc.).

How then to avoid the loss of social capital through

immigration at a local level? Putnam points to the importance of local sources of community bonding and integration. In Ireland, there are at least two:

1. The Catholic church (not very palatable to many in the media, but the reality for the majority of citizens in Ireland).
2. The GAA: possibly even stronger than the Catholic church these days in rallying local energies and commitment.

But that's probably not enough given the waning incidence of church-going and the lack of familiarity with hurling and Gaelic football among immigrants. Putnam points to one other source of social cohesion between immigrants and host communities in the USA besides religion and sport, namely the army.

Should we therefore have conscription into Ireland's defence forces to create our own melting pot, especially among second generation immigrants? If not conscription then what about a wider concept of national service? What if instead of transition year, all secondary-level students went straight through to Leaving Cert and were then required to spend a year (away from home) doing national service in voluntary groups, charities, sports organisations or indeed the defence forces? It would break down social class barriers (probably more pervasive and damaging than ethnic differences right now), as well as integrating young people from all backgrounds into a shared experience. Denmark is one example of a small European country that has benefited from such a requirement of its young people.

Republika Irlandii

Even this, of course, is not a palliative for the 'costs' of immigration. In Britain, the debate on this issue is well under way, and it would seem that the ideology of multi-culturalism (which essentially asserts that the host population's culture is no more entitled to preference or support than the cultures of immigrants) appears effectively to be dead. As always, we have the opportunity to learn from Britain's mistakes. A focus on belonging and opportunities for first generation and 'n'th generation descendents of immigrants to Ireland to share formative experiences together, will help.

Immigration and the naturalisation of some immigrants as Irish citizens has the potential for long-term, positive gains for Ireland. We are becoming a more culturally open country at a time when we need – more than ever – to rethink our place in the world and reshape our global economic relations. And the energy, enthusiasm and – yes – patriotism of these new Irish citizens will ultimately be part of the new narrative about Ireland and our future.

Perhaps because of our own experiences of emigration, we have been comparatively tolerant of immigration to Ireland. A recent Eurobarometer survey asked people all over Europe about the two most important issues they felt faced their individual countries. Needless to say, the economic situation and unemployment predominated – in Ireland as well as throughout the EU. But only 4 percent of adults in Ireland thought that immigration was one of the two biggest issues facing Ireland, down from 5 percent a year previously (the EU average is 9 percent).[5]

The Irish are a tolerant people by and large. We tend to berate ourselves about our health service, our litter and our weather – often ignoring the good things about our country. Among the positives is our extraordinary degree of tolerance. Take the findings about Ireland in a report on discrimination in the European Union from 2008. On measure after measure (from a survey sample of the total population) we are more tolerant than the twenty-seven member countries of the EU (EU27) as a whole on indicators such as:

- actual experience of discrimination on grounds of ethnic origin, sexual orientation, age, gender, religious belief and disability
- level of comfort with neighbours from different ethnic groups, etc. (with the notable exception of Roma)
- support for positive discrimination measures in the workplace
- having friends or acquaintances from different backgrounds (especially religious)[6]

By far the most powerful measure of our tolerance is the way in which we have responded to the extraordinary speed and scale of immigration to our country over the past ten years or so. The majority of Irish people consider immigration to have been a good thing on balance for Ireland, according to a nationwide survey in 2008 by Amárach Research.[7] Almost no other country has experienced such a surge in the share of foreign nationals in its total population (to over 10 percent in just ten years) with so little real social, economic or political strife as Ireland. There is no greater testimony to our tolerance as a people in my opinion. That said, the recession has meant that most Irish people want a stop to further immigration (though not necessarily for existing immigrants to go 'home'): 66 percent of Irish citizens want immigration policy to be more restrictive in the future.[8]

> In the 2016 Survey, only 4 percent of Irish people thought it likely Ireland would have its first Muslim president by 2020, and over two-thirds (68 percent) said they would not like it to happen.

We have to negotiate difficult times ahead. Economic uncertainty is adding to the challenge. Writers like Robert Putnam are suggesting that countries like Ireland need to find their own version of *E Pluribus Unum*. In other words we need a definition of Irishness for the twenty-first century that goes beyond platitudes and that makes the case for what makes us different (e.g. Ireland's cultural heritage), as well as what makes us the same (e.g. our membership of the European Union along with 400 million others). Ultimately debates about immigration and integration are about values – not economics, or politics or rights. Our tolerance is founded on the values that have made Ireland what it is today – a western mixture of Christianity, Ancient Greek philosophy (much of it via Muslim and Jewish thinkers) and our own Celtic heritage of course.

So the key task in anticipating the future course of immigration and integration in Ireland is one of gauging the course of our values in the coming years and, indeed, generations. As such, the issue transcends the normal left-right political spectrum, though maybe the adjustment is harder for those on the left (because of their championing of multi-culturalism in recent decades and its potential conflict with, say, cultural nationalism). Left-leaning writer David Goodhart has observed that 'a belief in universal moral equality does not mean that we have the same obligations to all humans'. He explains it thus:

> Until a few decades ago, the basis of national 'specialness' would have been ethnicity – shared ancestry, history, sacrifice. In multi-ethnic and multi-racial societies, the basis of specialness is citizenship itself. The justification for giving priority to the interests of fellow citizens boils down to a pragmatic claim about the value of the nation-state. Without fellow-citizen favouritism, the nation-state ceases to have much meaning. And most of the things that liberals desire – democracy, redistribution, welfare states, human rights – only work when one can assume the shared norms and solidarities of national communities.[9]

Adding to the challenge is the cultural interaction between immigrants and the host population, and the inevitable negotiation of values that such interaction gives rise to.

Not only is Ireland being changed by immigration, it was (and is) changing itself as a country by becoming a post-Christian, secular society – regardless of trends in immigration. That makes for a much more complex debate – one comprising intrinsic and extrinsic sources of change in fundamental values. The task then is to equip ourselves with the tools to accommodate this change even as the change is already under way. I believe that the intrinsic tolerance, compassion and wisdom of the Irish people will enable us to successfully negotiate the turbulent times ahead, and with openness as well – these things are best not done in secrecy or conspiratorially. Values are the cement that bind a people together – that make us feel that we belong.

But if facing the challenges of 2016 must be done out in the open, what then of the means we choose to convince others of the need to respond to these challenges?

Hidden Persuaders

The art of persuasion was something that mattered greatly to the signatories of the 1916 Proclamation. What had been secret up until Easter Monday was revealed to an unsuspecting public (and a somewhat more suspecting Dublin Castle), with a view to enlisting widespread support for the Rising. The Proclamation itself was a very overt form of written communication, but this choice of medium was not just confined to the Proclamation. The rebels managed to produce several editions of the *Irish War News*, handwritten by Pearse whilst in the GPO and printed by a friendly printer. The Easter Rising was also the occasion for the world's first ever radio news broadcast (in that the message was not destined for one ship or recipient as was the norm until then, but for anyone listening) from the Wireless School of Telegraphy across O'Connell Street from the GPO. For some twenty-four hours, the rebels broadcast the message in morse code:

> Irish Republic declared in Dublin today. Irish troops have captured city and are in full possession. Enemy cannot move in city. The whole country rising.[10]

It was not the first wartime message to exaggerate the true status of the sender.

Nevertheless, as we look to 2016, we can anticipate a rapidly changing world in terms of the art of persuasion and influence. We are witnessing the emergence of what futurist James Ogilvy called the 'advertising dividend' in a memorable essay entitled 'Earth Might Be Fair'.[11] This is what he envisaged:

> Imagine a world where all the resources now devoted to advertising were instead devoted to quality improvements in products. Just as we are now learning to live in a world where the Cold War is over and we can entertain the distribution of a peace dividend, imagine a time when we could entertain the distribution of … an advertising dividend.
>
> But what would all the … advertising and copywriters do? … Let them play. I'm serious … At risk of gross over-simplification I want to say that our most vexing problems today are not problems that can be solved by science and technology; they are problems that call for a degree of social invention that we have not seen since the creation of democracy … We don't yet know how to organise our human interactions.
>
> Despite the wonders of modern science there never seems to be enough: enough love, enough attention, enough respect, enough dignity … I know of no law of the constant conservation of laughter, or any limitation on joy. I see no reason to limit our sense of what is possible for the distribution of delight … Quite the contrary, there

might be a virtuous circle of mutual reinforcement in the spread of sublime delight, like a ripple of laughter that gains momentum in a crowd. According to the economics of the sublime, there can be enough for all.

The essay was written nearly twenty years ago and much of what Ogilvy foresaw is happening. The emergence of social networking via the internet has found a way to free up the advertising dividend, to better 'organise our human interactions'. New communication tools such as Facebook, instant messaging and texting have been adopted with gusto by the Irish, especially the young. To my mind this is something wonderful to behold, and it presages as radical a change to communications as was heralded by that first radio news broadcast in 1916.

This matters greatly to those seeking to influence the attitudes and behaviours of others. Whether as consumers or as voters, Irish people still prefer Irish media – TV, radio or press – to UK media, even though the majority of Irish people have easy access to the latter. This partly reflects the greater depth of coverage and insight into Irish developments by media based in Ireland. It is also a legacy of several generations brought up on Irish-only media choices in the days before satellite TV and the internet.

It is difficult, however, to imagine that the current generation of young people – and the next one – will have quite the same affinity for Irish media. Not only are they saturated in a mix of American and British content (soap operas, reality TV, music and celebrities), their viewing and reading choices are increasingly oriented away from Irish content.

The media world – and the wider world of culture and cultural content – may increasingly be divided less along national lines and more along linguistic lines. Take the internet: English was the number one language used in 2009 (some 480 million users), while Chinese was number two at over 380 million users.[12] Given that internet penetration is almost at saturation point in most English-speaking countries (though not India, if I can label it thus) and Chinese internet usage is still at an early stage of development, by 2016 we can expect Chinese to be the dominant language online. Internet penetration in Ireland will have peaked at around 90 percent by then, driven by mobile phone access. The internet will be the primary organisational channel not just for businesses but also for governments (vis-à-vis their citizens), for families, for voluntary groups and for political activists.

In the 2016 Survey, we asked whether people thought that different institutions, trends etc., would become more or less influential in the lives of Irish people by 2020.

Those institutions and factors expected to become influential (on balance) in the future include the European Commission, China, foreign companies, younger generations, and – especially – the internet.

Those institutions and trends expected to become less influential (on balance) in the future lives of Irish people include the Irish government, local authorities, trade unions, daily newspapers, RTÉ and – especially – the Catholic church.

Globally speaking, political activists include those 'secret revolutionary organisations' less intent nowadays on freedom and more on domination. Ireland's Institute of International and European Affairs has published a study on *Countering Militant Islamist Radicalisation on the Internet*.[13] It notes:

> Violent radicalisation on the internet is at the nexus of two key trends: the democratisation of communications driven by user generated content on the internet; and the democratisation of strategic violence driven by mass-casualty non-state terrorism. How best can Europe capitalise on the first trend to counter the second?

The study's author, Johnny Ryan, notes the drawbacks of censorship as one response to the threat and instead suggests:

> ... the chat rooms and web forums frequented by prospective militants and sympathisers can be exploited to promote division and disharmony. The internet, which is increasingly driven by user-made content and horizontal communication, rather than top-down content and passive receivers, provides an opportunity to engage with and challenge the militant Islamist justifications of violence in the very same venues where they are posted. The user-driven internet is well suited to a counter mobilisation against violent radicals for the same reason that it accommodated the call to violence in the same place: the internet is a passive venue where individuals do not simply receive messages. As illustrated by the growth of internet services such as Wikipedia, which are wholly reliant on the user to create their content, the internet is now an active venue, where users contribute to, adapt, and delete etc., content horizontally.[14]

If anything, it is the *lack* of secrecy on the internet that makes it a better tool for the advancement of freedom and democracy than for the advancement of violence and domination.

WHOSE ARMY?

The Easter Rising was famously 'called off' by Eoin MacNeill via an advertisement in the *Sunday Independent* on 23 April 1916. Today an organiser anxious to get a message to as many people as possible, as quickly as possible, would as likely use Facebook to reach his or her younger members, and even the not so young. Today the vast majority of Irish 18–24-year-olds use social networking sites on an almost daily basis.

There is something else happening, on an even bigger scale – nothing less than a redefinition of our evolved, human sense of belonging. The anthropologist Robin Dunbar hypothesised back in the 1990s that humans had evolved to live in communities of about 150 people. But 'digital prosthetics', such as Twitter and Facebook, may enable us to extend the Dunbar number to many hundreds more if not thousands, or 'ambient awareness' as social scientists now call it.[15]

I do think something profound is going on in terms of our experience of being human. If our sense of belonging is going to be replaced by ambient awareness – and three degrees of separation from everybody else online – then what are the implications for politics, for nation-states, and, indeed, for national identities? I expect it will be a mix of good and bad consequences.

The bad consequences may be more evident at first. Not least, the loss of privacy that inevitably follows logging and sharing so much of our lives online (in terms of daily content of our communications, work and family lives etc.). But these are early days for a still quite young medium and writers like Clay Shirky are right to suggest it will take fifty years or more for us to really understand the full impact of the changes now underway.[16] There may be other, negative consequences as well: increasing loneliness, for example, as people substitute virtual social lives for real ones. Even more disturbing is the potential for governments to use the internet to suppress dissent, as evident in China and Iran, for example.

Over the longer term, the more positive consequences of this new era should become more evident, especially the power to cheaply and effectively coordinate the inputs of many others, to an extent unimaginable by the IRB conspirators of 1916. Only there will be less conspiracy and more collaboration. Take the response of people to appeals from charities responding to humanitarian disasters: giving money and inviting others to help has never been easier. Nowadays you can raise an army (or a platoon) of helpers and supporters and funders in less time and for considerably less cost than ever before.

Such powers will give Ireland a global reach that we are only beginning to explore as a nation, powers that will help us forge a new 'destiny' in the years and decades ahead.

OUR EXILED CHILDREN

David McWilliams thinks we should do more to exploit the economic and business potential of the Irish diaspora, just as the Israelis have successfully exploited the Jewish diaspora. He was instrumental in establishing the Global Irish Economic Forum held in Farmleigh in 2009.[17] The GIEF initiative has the potential to contribute significantly in the decades ahead, judging by the impact of similar initiatives in other countries.

Look, for example, at the success of Israeli IT companies, the result of spin-offs from Israel's military sector. Ireland plainly doesn't have a strong military sector, but if the next generation of Irish IT entrepreneurs are to play to our strengths then what are they? The answer is obvious: it is our ability to network. Look at Irish usage of mobile phones or games consoles or social networks like Facebook. On many measures, we are actually ahead of most European countries (and certainly the United States when it comes to mobile phone usage).

Much of our use of technology is due to our culture and disposition as a people ('the greatest talkers since the Greeks' and all that). The international success of the iconic Irish pub plays to this sense of the loquacious, communicative, garrulous Irish and it even helps with our various diplomatic efforts on the world stage when we're seen as English speakers without the (US/British) baggage. All of this is to say that Irish IT entrepreneurs focusing on the networked future will at least be able to draw on the patterns and passions of their home market.

It is in that rich, breathtaking interface between design, technology and the future that the greatest opportunity for the next generation of successful Irish IT businesses lies. What is a diaspora if not a potential network just waiting to be connected?

Perfecting Our Discipline

Ireland needs to be disciplined in order to face the new challenges of the twenty-first century. But the disciplines we must perfect are very different indeed to those of the 1916 rebels. Take innovation: future job and wealth creation in Ireland will require that we champion innovation by Irish businesses in order to secure a higher standard of living for the Irish people. To be innovative is to be creative. And we Irish can be very creative. Nevertheless, setting targets for creativity is a bit like setting a target for how much you're going to enjoy the weekend. You can come up with a number – but usually you know creativity (and a good weekend) when you see it, whatever the score.

But if you are going to commit taxpayers' money to an innovation policy then some targets are necessary – such as those set out in the Forfás report on 'Skills in Creativity, Design and Innovation'.[18] It is a good primer on current thinking about innovation, creativity, etc., and the suggested targets are fair enough as far as they go.

But we need to go further: the real issue at the heart of creativity and innovation is the issue of risk. Doing nothing is often safer than doing something – in the private sector as well as the public sector. Right now Ireland is reverting to a more traditional 'risk averse' mode of thinking and doing. And who can blame us? Ireland is a country that imprisons people for not paying their TV licence, as well as having an exceptionally high level of personal guarantees demanded by banks from their business borrowers. Is it any wonder that demand for business loans has fallen off a cliff in Ireland even as it picks up elsewhere?

We are not alone in our new-found risk aversion – but that does not mean we are safe. Germany is falling behind many other countries in terms of its investment in innovation and creativity, although it would be nice to have their 'problems' (namely an economy that has fared much better than Ireland's in the course of the global recession).[19] We need to avoid being too specific about targets relating to innovation (including things like the spending on research and development as a percentage of GDP). Fetishising numbers is a highly uncreative thing to do. Moreover, fetishising innovation targets is no guarantee of economic success – Finland has not been insulated from the severity of the global economic recession by its previous investments in innovation strategy.

But Ireland can be innovative and creative without jeopardising our future wealth. Part of perfecting our discipline in this regard will entail creating a better environment for risk taking (of the non economy-wrecking kind), than setting spurious targets. And it will be more fun as well.

I think our advantage as Irish people is our openness –

brought about by being a small nation crucially dependent on trade, our use of the English language and easy absorption of US culture (the good and the bad), and our tolerant values that make us comfortable dealing with most people in most parts of the world without a whole lot of baggage. All of which, of course, is a consequence of our history and culture.

The Right Moment

The ancient Greeks had two concepts of time: *chronos* and *kairos*. The former is what we usually mean by time – the dimension linking the past to the present to the future. But *kairos* is different:

> *Kairos* (καιρός) is an ancient Greek word meaning the right or opportune moment (the supreme moment) … a time in between, a moment of an undetermined period of time in which something special happens … While *chronos* is quantitative, *kairos* has a qualitative nature.[20]

The 1916 Rising took place in *kairos* time – 'she now seizes that moment' – that fleeting intersection of opportunity and action. We experience *kairos* as individuals and we experience it in the organisations we belong to. Even countries experience *kairos*, their 'moment in the sun' when struggle and fortune combine to create breakthrough transformations in a nation's destiny.

The 2016 celebrations will be an opportunity for reflection, and – perhaps – for regeneration. Every nation is conscious (though not always fully) of the sacrifices previous generations made, in peacetime and in war, to secure the freedoms and opportunities successive generations have enjoyed. So it will be in 2016. But anniversaries should not just be an occasion for gratitude. They should also be an occasion for reorientation; of stepping back from the constant flow of *chronos* to once again check our course and perhaps adjust it if we are unhappy with the direction in which we are heading.

Ireland has come a long way in the century following the 1916 Rising. We have had many victories, including surviving the turbulence of partition, a civil war, the Great Depression and the Second World War. Beyond surviving we have embraced the opportunities presented by membership of the United Nations and the European Union, and have contributed much to that extraordinary achievement which has in turn secured freedom, peace and prosperity for hundreds of millions of our fellow Europeans. We Irish are an old people but we are still a young nation (chronologically and at heart) and we have many strengths that can help us achieve much more as a people. Whatever we set out to achieve – including maintaining and building on previous successes – we can be more confident than ever of victory.

IDEAS FOR THE 2016 PROCLAMATION

The Irish remain a nation of belongers – and new peoples belong to Ireland nearly a century after 1916. New communications technologies both enable a depth and breadth of connection with others not possible before, as well as providing the resources to create new sources of wealth, both now and in the future. The same tools for creativity and connection will also help forge deeper, more meaningful connections with the Irish outside Ireland.

Therefore our Proclamation must recognise and inspire our capacity for belonging and connection; including the 'new' Irish and the Irish abroad, in recognition of their power to help us to achieve our destiny.

4

The Right of the People

We declare the right of the people of Ireland to the ownership of Ireland, and to the unfettered control of Irish destinies, to be sovereign and indefeasible. The long usurpation of that right by a foreign people and government has not extinguished the right, nor can it ever be extinguished except by the destruction of the Irish people.

A NATION OF OWNERS

We Irish like to own property – on both sides of the border. Some 75 percent of households own their own homes in the Republic of Ireland, only slightly higher than the 71 percent in Northern Ireland.[1] Home ownership has increased steadily in the Republic of Ireland – in the 1946 Census the figure was only 57 percent.[2] Indeed, Irish levels of home ownership are among the highest in Europe and well above the EU27 average of 65 percent (only in Germany do a majority rent their homes).[3] Moreover, nearly half (46 percent) of all Irish homeowners own their home outright without a mortgage.[4]

The ownership of property and land has resonated deeply with the Irish over time. This is partly a consequence of the dominance of rural life in our economy, culture and society until well into the twentieth century. It is also – inevitably perhaps – a consequence of our colonial heritage, and the long legacy of land disputes and evictions. The decades before the Easter Rising witnessed the Land War of the late 1870s to 1890s, culminating in the 1903 and 1909 Land Acts that saw the UK government provide loans to Irish tenants to buy their freeholds, including compulsory purchases in some instances (partly to 'kill Home Rule with kindness' as some historians have noted).[5]

This was the context for the rebels' declaration of 'the right of the people of Ireland to the ownership of Ireland'. Nearly 100 years later, such a right remains 'sovereign and indefeasible' in the eyes of most Irish people. At least, that is one interpretation. James Connolly – the only socialist signatory of the Proclamation – had a somewhat different interpretation:

> ... that 'property' has no rights as against the welfare of the community, and that the life and prosperity of the people is, or ought to be, the first care of statesmanship ... Property of all kinds ought to be subject to the community, and if the welfare of the community requires that 'legal' rights of property shall be subordinated, or even totally set aside, it must be done.[6]

Connolly's views were – and still are – in the minority when it comes to property rights in Ireland. But it wasn't just Connolly who foresaw tensions between private and public rights in relation to property. In his essay *The Sovereign People*, written one month before the Rising, Patrick Pearse observed that:

> To insist upon the sovereign control of the nation over all the property within the nation is not to disallow the right to private property. It

is for the nation to determine to what extent private property may be held by its members, and in what items of the nation's material resources private property shall be allowed. A nation may, for instance, determine, as the free Irish nation determined and enforced for many centuries, that private ownership shall not exist in land; that the whole of a nation's soil is the public property of the nation. A nation may determine, as many modern nations have determined, that all the means of transport within a nation, all its railways and waterways, are the public property of the nation to be administered by the nation for the general benefit. A nation may go further and determine that all sources of wealth whatsoever are the property of the nation, that each individual shall give his service for the nation's good, and shall be adequately provided for by the nation, and that all surplus wealth shall go to the national treasury to be expended on national purposes, rather than be accumulated by private persons.

There is nothing divine or sacrosanct in any of these arrangements; they are matters of purely human concern, matters for discussion and adjustment between the members of a nation, matters to be decided upon finally by the nation as a whole; and matters in which the nation as a whole can revise or reverse its decision whenever it seems good in the common interests to do so. I do not disallow the right to private property; but I insist that all property is held subject to the national sanction.[7]

For Pearse, as for Connolly, the trade-off involved means and ends. Or as Pearse put it in the same essay:

The whole is entitled to pursue the happiness and prosperity of the whole, but this is to be pursued exactly for the end that each of the individuals composing the whole may enjoy happiness and prosperity, the maximum amount of happiness and prosperity consistent with the happiness and prosperity of all the rest. One may reduce all this to a few simple propositions:

1. The end of freedom is human happiness.
2. The end of national freedom is individual freedom; therefore, individual happiness.
3. National freedom implies national sovereignty.
4. National sovereignty implies control of all the moral and material resources of the nation.

Pearse was more of an idealist than an ideologue, and he could not have foreseen (any more than Connolly could) the consequences later in the twentieth century when emerging ideologies distorted such sentiments to mean that enslavement to the state was 'freedom'. But the tension between ownership versus rights continues (as it does in most democracies). It is even reflected in Ireland's Constitution crafted in 1937.[8] Article 43 declaims:

1.1 The State acknowledges that man, in virtue of his rational being, has the natural right, antecedent to positive law, to the private ownership of external goods.

1.2 The State accordingly guarantees to pass no law attempting to abolish the right of private ownership or the general right to transfer, bequeath and inherit property.

On the other hand, the same article notes that:

2.1 The State recognises, however, that the exercise of the rights mentioned in the foregoing provisions of this Article ought, in civil society, to be regulated by the principles of social justice.

2.2 The State, accordingly, may as occasion requires delimit by law
the exercise of the said rights with a view to reconciling their
exercise with the exigencies of the common good.

In recent years, there has been considerable discussion about some
of the more perverse consequences of Ireland's constitutional
protection for property rights. The All Party Oireachtas
Committee on the Constitution published its Ninth Progress
Report specifically on the topic of Private Property in 2004.[9] As
part of their review, the committee was asked to consider:

> ... the need for updating provisions which pertain to planning
> controls and infrastructural development. In its examination of
> the Articles relating to property the committee was particularly
> concerned, therefore, to establish whether the balance struck in
> them between the rights of the individual and the exigencies of the
> common good was such as to impose unnecessary impediments to
> legislation which would either control or otherwise regulate the price
> of building land on the one hand or which would seek to eliminate
> many of the obstacles to the speedy roll-out of major infrastructural
> projects on the other hand.

The report itself then went on to examine in detail issues such
as the dynamics of the Irish property market, and in particular
how the planning system affected it. It addressed criticisms of
the planning system, setting out recommendations on zonings
and re-zonings, development control and consent, provision of
infrastructure, provisions for compulsory purchase and rural
housing. It was, of course, 'too little too late' in terms of heading

off the unprecedented speculative pressures then driving the property bubble that engulfed Ireland in the 2000s.

Nevertheless, even with the introduction of changes recommended in different reports over several decades (including development levies and planning gain requirements), property rights in Ireland remain very strong. The Heritage Foundation lists property rights as one of ten components of its *Index of Economic Freedom*, describing it thus:

> The property rights component is an assessment of the ability of individuals to accumulate private property, secured by clear laws that are fully enforced by the state. It measures the degree to which a country's laws protect private property rights and the degree to which its government enforces those laws. It also assesses the likelihood that private property will be expropriated and analyses the independence of the judiciary, the existence of corruption within the judiciary, and the ability of individuals and businesses to enforce contracts. The more certain the legal protection of property, the higher a country's score; similarly, the greater the chances of government expropriation of property, the lower a country's score.

Ireland is given a score of ninety out of one hundred in relation to property rights – as high as any other developed democracy anywhere in the world.[10] But whilst our property rights remain strong nearly a century after their sovereignty was proclaimed by the 1916 rebels, our appetite for property ownership may well wane significantly by 2016.

Renting the Future

Many older Americans, born in the 1930s, are in the habit of keeping cash in their homes, under the mattress so to speak. No doubt this is a consequence of their having lived through the Great Depression and witnessing over 3,000 banks fail, wiping out a generation's savings in the process. Such formative experiences in our youth tend to shape our values and behaviours over the rest of our lives, long after the formative experiences have passed.

Here in Ireland, a generation of young people under thirty will never look at property the same way again as a result of what they are now experiencing – and will experience over the next few years. This is not a storm that will pass, loosening a few slates on the roof. Rather, we are experiencing an earthquake that will transform key features of Ireland's economic landscape beyond recognition. As with all such economic upheavals there are social, political and cultural consequences as well. One such consequence will likely be a permanent demise in the Irish love affair – infatuation even – with property ownership, especially debt-funded ownership. The wave of the future may well be to rent – not just property but also furniture, clothes, cars, etc. Renting is the new buying.

The appetite for ownership is a function of scarcity: when ownership is effectively the only guarantee of access to the benefits of a particular product or service then other arrangements (such as renting or sharing) are grossly inferior. But when the supply of something becomes abundant – even excessive relative to underlying demand – then ownership becomes unnecessary. We do not own the roads we drive on or the world wide web that we surf, yet we have more or less unlimited access to all we want when we want it, for now anyway. An ironic consequence of the recent failures of finance-fuelled capitalism may well be to undermine forever the foundational faith in private property ownership as a source of wealth and freedom (although 'ironic' doesn't quite do justice to such an outcome).

The recession that started in 2008 is turning out to be Ireland's first middle-class recession – professionals are joining unskilled workers on the dole queues. If anything, it is the Irish middle classes who are bearing the brunt of this recession, as they are the ones with the most debt and lifestyles typically geared to rely on both the incomes of working couples. Long gone are the days of a middle class comprising working husbands and stay-at-home mums; since 2001 the majority of married women of working age in Ireland have been in paid employment. That was how the middle class fuelled the expansion of the buy-to-let market, aided and abetted by our over-leveraged banks.

Such are the seismic economic and social shifts now underway. Indeed the traditional snobbery and stigma associated with renting ('a waste of money' as they used to say before the onset of industrial-scale negative equity), will disappear faster than 100 percent mortgage offers. The 2016 centenary will not see the return of the tenement slums that plagued Dublin in the early twentieth century, but it may see a reversal of the trend towards property ownership that followed in the wake of independence.

Selfless government

How 'sovereign' can a sovereign country be in the twenty-first century? And does sovereignty still mean what it meant in Pearse's time?

> National independence involves national sovereignty. National sovereignty is twofold in its nature. It is both internal and external. It implies the sovereignty of the nation over all its parts, over all men and things within the nation; and it implies the sovereignty of the nation as against all other nations.[11]

To what extent can these ideals be relevant in 2016? Futurist Daniel Bell once observed that 'the nation-state is becoming too small for the big problems of life, and too big for the small problems of life'.[12] And there is some truth in the observation that globalisation has created an entirely new dynamic for nation-states. Indeed, the last great globalisation – before the First World War – took place during the peak of European empires: there were far fewer nation-states back in 1916.

The years since 1916 have witnessed an extraordinary flowering of nation-states as empires declined and withdrew. At the start of the Great War there were some forty-five independent nation-states worldwide. As of 2010, there are over 200 nation-states. There is little to suggest there will be any fewer by 2016. Clearly the nation-state is a winning political structure. National independence appears to have widespread appeal, despite the pressures Bell and others are concerned with.

Immanuel Wallerstein, writing in 1997, had a remarkably similar view to Pearse about the nature of sovereignty, even if he had a distinctly more left-wing view of its origins and purpose:

> What then are the peculiarities of the modern state? First and foremost, that it claims sovereignty. Sovereignty, as it has been defined since the sixteenth century, is a claim not about the state but about the interstate system. It is a double claim, looking both inward and outward. Sovereignty of the state, inward-looking, is the assertion that, within its boundaries (which therefore must necessarily be clearly defined and legitimated within the interstate system) the state may pursue whatever policies it deems wise, decree whatever laws it deems necessary, and that it may do this without any individual, group, or sub state structure inside the state having the right to refuse to obey the laws. Sovereignty of the state, outward-looking, is the argument that no other state in the system has the right to exercise any authority, directly or indirectly, within the boundaries of the given state, since such an attempt would constitute a breach of the given state's sovereignty. No doubt, earlier state forms also claimed authority within their realms, but 'sovereignty' involves in addition the mutual recognition of these claims of the states within an interstate system. That is, sovereignty in the modern world is a reciprocal concept.[13]

But Wallerstein notes there are obvious problems with the 'Pearsean' ideal:

> However, as soon as we put these claims on paper, we see immediately how far they are from a description of how the modern world really works. No modern state has ever been truly inwardly sovereign de facto, since there has always been internal resistance to its authority.

Indeed in most states this resistance has led to institutionalising legal limitations on internal sovereignty in the form, among others, of constitutional law. Nor has any state even been truly outwardly sovereign, since interference by one state in the affairs of another is common currency, and since the entire corpus of international law (admittedly a weak reed) represents a series of limitations on outward sovereignty. In any case, strong states notoriously do not reciprocate fully recognition of the sovereignty of weak states.

Ireland has, on balance, fared well from globalisation in the late twentieth and early twenty-first centuries. We have one of the most open economies in the world (as indicated, for example, by the share of trade in Irish GDP). Ireland's membership of the European Union and the eurozone points to a commitment to openly engage in international forums supportive of open trade and its benefits. But our openness is potentially also a threat: our fortunes are tied to global forces that are far beyond our control.

Nor has trade been the main or only motivation for our participation in bodies like the United Nations. In his capacity as Minister for External Affairs, Eamon de Valera won admiration for his work at the League of Nations, where he was president of both the council and the assembly of the League in 1932 and 1938 respectively. De Valera was particularly concerned with the prospects for small countries against a background of growing threats to many such countries in Europe and Asia. Long before the European Union and the eurozone came into existence, de Valera saw the value of international co-operation as a means of securing lasting peace and prosperity, even as he lamented the failure of many of his contemporaries to understand this on the eve of the Second World War:

> Why cannot the nations put into the enterprises of peace the energy they are prepared to squander in the futility and frightfulness of war? Yesterday there were no finances to give the workless the opportunity of earning their bread; tomorrow, money unlimited will be found to provide for the manufacture of instruments of destruction.
>
> Why can we not, in the spirit of justice, deal with wrongs when we perceive them? ... Or will our conservatism, the natural philosophy of those who have and are concerned only to retain – will this conservatism give its consent and deem the time right only when the slaughter has begun? Are adjustments never to be made but at the expense of the weak?[14]

In the 2016 Survey, we asked whether people agreed or disagreed that *I am proud of Ireland's achievements as an independent nation*?

Three in four Irish people (74 percent) agreed they are proud, 41 percent of them 'agreed strongly'. Agreement was strongest among over 55-year-olds, and those in higher social class groups. Only 9 percent disagreed – 4 percent 'disagreed strongly'.

TOO SMALL TO SUCCEED

Daniel Bell's challenge remains, however. Is Ireland, like many of the other nations that secured their independence over the course of the twentieth century, no longer 'fit for purpose'? In other words, are we too small for the big issues, and too big for the small issues?

There has been much debate about the future of nation-states in the years since Bell and others raised such issues. The expansion of the European Union – including the successful introduction of the euro – has required a 'pooling of sovereignty' by participating countries in certain critical areas. So have we rejected the idea that control of Ireland's destiny is 'sovereign and indefeasible'? Of course not. Our destiny has not been 'usurped' by 'a foreign people and government'. Instead we have chosen as a sovereign people to freely secure the benefits of participation in a wider European Union along with other sovereign peoples willing to share in the same benefits.

In a speech commemorating the ninetieth anniversary of the First Dáil, Taoiseach Brian Cowen noted:

> Experiences such as this have helped us to understand the true meaning of our country's sovereignty: that properly understood, it means independence of action, not insularity; and that while in theory all states enjoy unfettered sovereignty, in practice, the real freedom available to an individual country to chart its own course in the world may be rather less.
>
> Since 1973 therefore, we have applied this principle to guide our participation in what is now the European Union. Our membership puts Ireland squarely at the centre of one of the world's most influential players. Amplified by the Union, Ireland's voice, unlike that of the First Dáil, can no longer be ignored internationally. In 1919 terms, not only are our requests now heard by the Great Powers; we are sitting regularly around the table with many of them as equals. On six occasions we have presided over their meetings, most recently in 2004, at the head of a Union of almost 500 million people.
>
> Our influence within the Union is pervasive, whether at the

highest levels of its institutions, or as a mediator helping to resolve different positions at inter-governmental meetings. We have been extremely successful participants in the Union and it has given us a reach and a power unachievable to us alone.

In short, our membership of the Union gives life to the aspirations of the First Dáil …

The truth is that Europe empowers us. It gives us a place at the table, from which we can deploy our resources, our influence and our sovereignty to the benefit of the Irish people.

That, ultimately, was the goal of the first Dáil: to empower the Irish people to elect Irish men and women to an Irish parliament to serve their best interests honestly and unselfishly …

Alongside peace and a respected place at the heart of Europe, together we have also used our independence to build a stronger, fairer Ireland.[15]

On balance, the vast majority of Irish people are quite content with Ireland's experiences of pooling sovereignty with other countries in the European Union. Despite the economic crisis and two referenda on the Lisbon Treaty, the Irish remain among the most enthusiastic members of the European Union. In a pan-EU poll by Eurobarometer in late 2009, some 72 percent of Irish people agreed that membership of the EU was generally a good thing (versus an EU27 average of 53 percent); and an even higher percentage – 81 percent – felt that Ireland had, on balance, benefited from membership of the EU (57 percent average for the EU27 countries).[16] Moreover, a slightly higher percentage of Irish people in the same survey were more satisfied with the way democracy works in the European Union (60 percent) than were satisfied with the way democracy works in Ireland itself (56 percent) – still above the EU27 average in both instances.

But where might a process of pooling sovereignty end? Critics of such a process (not just in Ireland), fear that the ultimate destination is a European 'Super State'; perhaps as a precursor to a 'World Government'. Such notions seem fanciful at present, if only because there appears to be little appetite on the part of large countries to cede any more sovereignty or to be subject to yet more binding international agreements. Witness, for example, the failure of the Copenhagen conference on climate change at the end of 2009. If anything, the financial crisis of 2008–2009 has enhanced rather than diminished the powers of nation-states, not just relative to international bodies, but also relative to the multinational businesses many had feared were becoming stronger than national governments. This especially applies to banks, of course. Indeed, as we approach 2016, the sovereign nation-state appears to be in robust good health, better even than might have been imagined by the 1916 rebels, living as they were in the age of empires.

But if the momentum for the submergence of nation-states into super-states appears to have halted (and maybe even been reversed), what about momentum in the other direction? Is Ireland, for example, closer to the 'optimum' state size for the twenty-first century? One recent review of state size in the twentieth and twenty-first centuries by Kurt Taylor Gaubatz concluded:

> There will always be idiosyncrasies that affect optimal size for any given state – natural defensive boundaries and communications

barriers such as mountain ranges and oceans, the distribution of ethnic groupings, accidents of history, and the like. But there are also larger factors that change over time.

In three critical functional areas – economics, national security and human rights – the incentives for large state size are diminishing. The creation of regional and global regimes to provide services that require large economies of scale creates an environment in which the most fundamental modalities of political organisation can now gravitate to a lower level. If the stickiness of historically enshrined boundaries can be overcome, we can expect the twenty-first century to be a period of increasing fragmentation within the context of an increasingly polycentric international system.

The dynamics of integration and fragmentation are intimately connected: the development of institutions and norms at the international level can change the politics and economics for the provision of critical public goods. When certain public goods such as security and the enforcement of open trading rules can be provided on a more global scale, there will be considerable pressure for the fragmentation of political institutions in the remaining areas of governance. By this logic, we are likely to see a continued devolution of power to the regional, and even the local level, as this century unfolds.[17]

But we have already noted Ireland's 'surfeit' of government in Chapter 1. Is Ireland perhaps 'small enough' to meet the criteria for a successfully functioning sovereign state in the twenty-first century? The last time the island of Ireland was a single, political entity was under British rule. In 1916, Ireland – north and south – had 103 MPs in the British House of Commons. Since 1921, there have been two distinct and separate political entities on our small island. Instead of two, would we better off with four or ten or thirty-two? Some of the most successful economies are those which are not so much nation-states as city-states: Singapore, Luxembourg and Hong Kong, for example.

In the 2016 Survey, we asked whether people agreed or disagreed that *In the long run small countries like Ireland will disappear as only bigger countries will be able to deal with the challenges of the future?*

The majority of Irish people (54 percent) disagreed, 34 percent of them 'strongly'. Disagreement was strongest among those living in Dublin. Just over one in five (22 percent) agreed, strongest among 35–44-year-olds.

The 1916 rebels proclaimed the indefeasibility of the ownership and control of Ireland. Their focus was on devolving power to the nation from the empire, rather than on devolving power to local communities from central government. And yet the principle of subsidiarity evokes such a possibility. Subsidiarity is best defined as the idea that a central authority should have a subsidiary function, performing only those tasks which cannot be performed effectively at a more immediate or local level. Subsidiarity is an established feature of EU law and has been formalised in a number of treaties. For example, the 1992 Treaty on European Union states that:

> In areas which do not fall within its exclusive competence, the Community shall take action, in accordance with the principle of subsidiarity, only if and in so far as the objectives of the proposed

action cannot be sufficiently achieved by the Member States and can therefore, by reason of the scale or effects of the proposed action, be better achieved by the Community.[18]

But the principle of subsidiarity does not just apply to national governments and their relationships with international bodies such as the European Union. It also applies to regional, local and community governance within a nation-state. By 2016, we will see increasing tensions within the Republic of Ireland due to fundamental economic and demographic trends that pose very different challenges for different parts of the country. As the seminal 2008 report from DIT's Futures Academy, *Twice the Size: Imagineering the Future of Ireland's Gateways,* observed:

> The basic conclusion emerging from these drivers is that by the year 2030 over two-thirds of the population of the island of Ireland will be concentrated within 25 km of the east coast. There is no evidence that existing strategies will prevent this, nor indeed is there any evidence that this would be desirable. An eastern corridor from Belfast to Waterford, is likely to be Ireland's best opportunity to maintain a competitive position among the city-regions of an increasingly competitive Europe.[19]

This raises profound implications for the future 'control of Irish destinies'. The 1916 rebels would not have concerned themselves with regional prospects – other than the challenge posed by unionist hostility, primarily in the north, to Home Rule (never mind independence). And yet Ireland's future success beyond 2016 will require an attention to regional development that will raise issues about subsidiarity and sovereignty that will create tensions as emotional – though hopefully not as violent – as those posed by northern dissension in 1916. The conclusion of *Twice the Size* notes:

> It is necessary to provide all Irish cities and regions with ample development opportunities, but in a way that will reinforce and strengthen the already existing critical mass on the east coast, not impede it? The success of the east is and will be the success of the whole country if the future of these places is to be viewed in the context of complementarity with the east and not competition.

The future of Irish sovereignty – beyond 2016 – will as likely be debated in terms of national-regional dynamics as global-national ones. The people of Ireland will, for the most part, continue to control their destiny, but it will be anything but 'unfettered'.

IDEAS FOR THE 2016 PROCLAMATION

The concept of national sovereignty inspired many more nations to seek independence after the 1916 Rising. But sovereignty – and the control over collective destiny that it implies – means something more in the twenty-first century. It means both the sharing and the distribution of control at levels other than the nation-state where appropriate.

Therefore our new Proclamation must reframe the meaning of sovereignty to reflect the integrated and diverse complexities of the twenty-first century.

5

Exaltation Among the Nations

In every generation the Irish people have asserted their right to national freedom and sovereignty; six times during the last three hundred years they have asserted it in arms. Standing on that fundamental right and again asserting it in arms in the face of the world, we hereby proclaim the Irish Republic as a Sovereign Independent State, and we pledge our lives and the lives of our comrades-in-arms to the cause of its freedom, of its welfare, and of its exaltation among the nations.

A POSTER CHILD NO MORE

Until recently, Ireland was a country others wanted to emulate. We were the 'poster child' for successful, orthodox economic development, and an example to others of how to raise a nation out of failure and poverty. Our exaltation among the nations – as a role model for others to follow – seemed assured. But not any more. Indeed, Ireland is increasingly held up as an example of how badly things can go wrong.

Our fall from grace seems set to continue to 2016 and beyond as the consequences of economic mismanagement reverberate down through the generations. But all is not lost. We are still a comparatively young nation – in spirit as well as demography.

That creates its own dynamic – one that can mitigate some of the harsher economic trends. Moreover, sometimes a nation is at its best in struggle – indeed, success did not rest easy on Irish shoulders (not that many had enough time to get used to it of course). We will struggle as a nation in the years ahead, but it is a struggle that will leave us older, wiser and in some ways better when it is done.

A Violent Past

The 1916 Rising took place against the background of the most violent international conflict ever experienced up to that point in world history. The First World War was the culmination of other violent conflicts in the late nineteenth century and first decade of the twentieth century, including the Franco-Prussian War of 1870–71, the Russo-Turkish War of 1877–78 and the Balkan Wars of 1912–13.

Yet the build-up to war in August 1914 was almost ignored in Ireland – preoccupied as the country was with increasingly militant tensions surrounding Home Rule, tensions that had already drawn blood when four civilians (among a group suspected of gun-running) were killed by British soldiers on Bachelor's Walk in Dublin in late July. Indeed, Britain's entry into the First World War was actually welcomed by some in Ireland as preventing a war at home.[1] Others welcomed the First World War because of its potential to accelerate the prospect of Irish freedom. Pearse observed in an addendum to *How Does She Stand?*, written in August 1914 as the war began:

A European war has brought about a crisis which may contain, as yet hidden within it, the moment for which the generations have been waiting. It remains to be seen whether, if that moment reveals itself, we shall have the sight to see and the courage to do, or whether it shall be written of this generation, alone of all the generations of Ireland, that it had none among it who dared to make the ultimate sacrifice.[2]

James Connolly was equally opportunistic:

The time is now ripe, nay, the imperious necessities of the hour call loudly for, demand, the formation of a Committee of all the earnest elements, outside as well as inside the Volunteers, to consider means to take and hold Ireland and the food of Ireland for the people of Ireland ...

Freedom, we believe, cannot flourish, or even awaken into life in the miasmatic atmosphere of wirepulling and intrigue, but as St Just said: 'Liberty is born in storm and tears as the Earth arose out of chaos, and as man comes wailing into the world.'

We, who have faced the storm for industrial liberty and wept the tears for the sufferings of our own class, will not shrink from either for the sake of our country. Try us![3]

The atmosphere of jingoism and militarism was not confined to Ireland and Britain, of course. All of Europe seemed swept up in the exhilaration of war, and a generation of Europeans that had known little violent conflict (other than on the margins such as in the Balkans), willingly took up arms against one another. It was 'the war to end all wars' – a noble means to a glorious end. Pearse reflected much of this in his own writings:

War is a terrible thing, and this is the most terrible of wars. But this war is not more terrible than the evils which it will end or help to end … What if the war sets Poland and Ireland free? If the war does these things, will not the war have been worthwhile? War is a terrible thing, but war is not an evil thing. It is the things that make war necessary that are evil. The tyrannies that wars break, the lying formulae that wars overthrow, the hypocrisies that wars strip naked, are evil.[4]

His belief in the potential for violence to secure a lasting peace was – tragically for some ten million men killed in the First World War – very much in keeping with the ethos of the time. It was a belief that survived that war and the even greater slaughter of the Second World War (which witnessed some sixty million deaths).

WE PLEDGE OUR LIVES

Could it happen again? Could a long peace, such as Europe has known since 1945, lull Europeans – including the Irish – into embracing the romance of war again? *Dulce et decorum est pro patria mori* (it is sweet and right to die for one's country), as millions believed at the start of the last century? It seems unlikely, even if there are many more countries to die for. We have learned to distinguish patriotism from nationalism, something George Orwell observed in the closing months of the Second World War:

Nationalism is not to be confused with patriotism. Both words are normally used in so vague a way that any definition is liable to be challenged, but one must draw a distinction between them, since two different and even opposing ideas are involved. By 'patriotism' I mean devotion to a particular place and a particular way of life, which one believes to be the best in the world but has no wish to force on other people. Patriotism is of its nature defensive, both militarily and culturally. Nationalism, on the other hand, is inseparable from the desire for power. The abiding purpose of every nationalist is to secure more power and more prestige, not for himself but for the nation or other unit in which he has chosen to sink his own individuality.[5]

The 1916 rebels were both nationalists – they desired the political power to govern Ireland – *and* patriots: they believed passionately in the uniqueness and beauty of Irish culture and traditions. Political violence is the shadow side of nationalism, even as freedom and independence are its pronounced goals. The criticism of nationalism as an ideology – which gathered pace as the number of nations expanded, especially after the Second World War – has focused on the issue of violence.

Critics of nationalism would point out that it has been the leading cause of both war and internal repression over the past hundred years. Nazism or 'National Socialism' justified the mass murder of those who were deemed enemies of Germany and the waging of war on neighbouring countries to create *lebensraum* (living space) for Germans. Likewise communism in its Russian, Chinese, Korean, Cuban and other varieties amounted to little more than national kleptocracies bent on robbing and suppressing their peoples at horrendous costs in terms of starvation and death.

Nationalism can also give rise to extremes of xenophobia, which can manifest itself as protectionism and in anti-immigrant politics. The nationalist world view, *in extremis*, is a zero-sum view: one which sees gains by other countries as losses for the nationalist's country, and vice versa. From such a critical perspective, nationalism – be it the Irish nationalism of Pearse or the national socialism of Hitler – must seemingly end in violence and evil, as the prize to be won entails taking what is held by others.

But such criticisms go too far. As with all potential sources of harm, the lethality of every poison is in the dosage. Nationalism, like religion, has been a force for peace, freedom and compassion as much as – if not more than – it has been a force for avoidable evil in the world. The appeal of nationhood down through the centuries has been one based not so much on a desire for revenge and repression (or possession), but rather a desire for freedom from repression and the freedom of a newly sovereign people to control their own destiny.

Experience would suggest that a patriotic sense of shared identity plays a vital, complementary role in democracies. Without a sense of 'us', democratic politics too quickly degenerates into 'majoritarianism', which brings its own risks of repression and even violence.[6] The history of Northern Ireland is testimony to this: here was a democratic state (within a larger, democratic state) that failed, until quite recently, to secure the democratic support of its Catholic, nationalist minority.

On balance, therefore, nationalism leavened by patriotism has proved a successful partner to democratic politics, though neither the future of nation-states nor of democracy should be taken for granted in the twenty-first century.

In the 2016 Survey we asked under what circumstances did people think it would be right for the Irish people to become involved in armed conflict. They were presented with three scenarios.

The first related to a scenario in which we were members of a UN peace-keeping force defending threatened peoples in other countries. Nearly half (48 percent) agreed that Irish people should become involved in an armed conflict of that nature. Significantly more men than women agreed (58 and 39 percent respectively), and more 35–54-year-olds than those in younger/older age groups.

The second scenario was one in which another EU country was invaded and all others were asked to come to their defence. Far fewer (34 percent) agreed that Irish people should become involved in an armed conflict of that nature. There were the same gender and age gaps.

The third scenario was one in which Ireland was invaded by a foreign army as part of a wider conflict. A much larger majority (68 percent) agreed that Irish people should become involved in an armed conflict in that event. The majority of both men and women (more of the latter than the former) agreed in this case.

Just under one in five (18 percent) Irish people felt that armed conflict would not be right in any of the three scenarios presented.

COMRADES-IN-ARMS

Despite the headlines, this is a comparatively peaceful century, so far. And despite the conflict in Northern Ireland, the Republic of Ireland has known uninterrupted peace since the end of the Civil War in May 1923. On most measures, Ireland is one of the most peaceful countries in the world. The 2009 Global Peace Index, for example, ranks Ireland as the twelfth most peaceful country in the world:

> The concept of peace is notoriously difficult to define. The simplest way of approaching it is in terms of harmony achieved by the absence of war or conflict. Applied to nations, this would suggest that those not involved in violent conflicts with neighbouring states or suffering internal wars would have achieved a state of peace. This is what Johan Galtung defined as a 'negative peace' – an absence of violence.[7]

Peace has a dual benefit to societies in that a) it means that valuable resources are not diverted to unproductive defence; and b) there is less risk associated with investments that ultimately create jobs and wealth. As the authors of the Global Peace Index observe:

> Peace creates the environment in which other activities that contribute to growth can take place. In this sense, it is a facilitator of growth, making it easier for workers to produce, businesses to sell, consumers to buy, entrepreneurs and scientists to innovate, and government to regulate. This concept could be labelled 'normal growth dynamics'. The assumption is that normal activities which contribute to growth and prosperity can be hindered by war and violence, even if the productive capacity itself exists. Thus, human capital, good infrastructure and open markets may be important factors in growth, but their contributions will be diminished or even eliminated if they are subject to violence and serious societal conflict.

Peace also frees up resources for productive activities which would otherwise be diverted to controlling or creating violence. This is true for material and human resources as well as for investment capital. Finally, peace creates a stable environment that is congenial to confidence and long-term planning. This then supports rational risk-taking, investment, employment, borrowing, and strategic planning, all of which are important to produce highly productive activity.[8]

Ireland continues to benefit from peace. One measure of the benefit is the United Nations Human Development Index (HDI). The HDI uses existing data sources to provide a composite measure of three dimensions of human development: living a long and healthy life (measured by life expectancy), being educated (measured by adult literacy and gross enrolment in education) and having a decent standard of living (measured by purchasing power parity incomes). The index's authors recognise that this is not a comprehensive measure of human development, and instead they argue that it provides a broad prism for viewing human progress and the complex relationship between income and well-being.

They have been tracking individual country HDI scores since 1990. The most recent HDI report for 2009 reports Ireland as having the fifth highest HDI score in the world, out of 182 countries covered by the study.[9] Ireland ranks eighteenth on measured life expectancy, tenth on educational measures and tenth on the standard of living score. Peace has indeed been good for Ireland.

Unlike 1914, when Europe seemed gripped by a blood lust after decades of relative calm, there appears at present to be no desire for war on the part of any major countries – democratic or otherwise. Indeed, some would argue that we live in exceptionally peaceful times compared to our ancestors, despite nightly news reports and impressions to the contrary. Stephen Pinker, for example, points out:

> We also have very good statistics for the history of one-on-one murder, because for centuries many European municipalities have recorded causes of death. When the criminologist Manuel Eisner scoured the records of every village, city, county and nation he could find, he discovered that homicide rates in Europe had declined from 100 killings per 100,000 people per year in the Middle Ages to less than one killing per 100,000 people in modern Europe.
>
> And since 1945 in Europe and the Americas, we've seen steep declines in the number of deaths from interstate wars, ethnic riots and military coups, even in South America. Worldwide, the number of battle deaths has fallen from 65,000 per conflict per year to less than 2,000 deaths in this decade. Since the end of the Cold War in the early 1990s, we have seen fewer civil wars, a 90 percent reduction in the number of deaths by genocide, and even a reversal in the 1960s-era uptick in violent crime.[10]

Why is this happening? Explanations range from better education (more people foreseeing the adverse consequences of violence), to better government (the democratic state as neutral referee and judge in disputes between neighbours), to changing 'valuations' of human life (it isn't 'cheap' any more), to expanding 'circles of empathy' (beyond family and tribe to nation and humanity). As Pinker suggests:

Whatever its causes, the decline of violence has profound implications. It is not a license for complacency. We enjoy the peace we find today because people in past generations were appalled by the violence in their time and worked to end it, and so we should work to end the appalling violence in our time.

It seems improbable that another generation of Irish people will be forced to assert their right to national freedom and sovereignty – especially asserting it in arms.

THE PRICE OF PEACE

The 1916 rebels believed that armed rebellion would ultimately secure peaceful independence for Ireland, just as their fellow Irishmen on the Western Front believed they were fighting for Home Rule. My grandfather, John Joseph O'Neill, was one of the latter. In 1914, at the age of seventeen (he pretended he was eighteen, as many under-aged boys did) he joined the Royal Inniskilling Fusiliers. He was one of over 17,000 Ulster Catholics who fought in the First World War, something that tends to be forgotten in the traditional Unionist narrative about Ulster and the war.[11] Indeed, there was widespread enthusiasm in both communities for the war, as illustrated in W.J. Canning's history of the 9th Battalion of the Fusiliers:

The whole country was in the grip of military fever and was edging very close to civil war where Irish National Volunteers and Ulster Volunteers were drilling in the same townlands. The outbreak of war brought these organisations out of this unthinkable situation to combine their energies in a common cause. The papers reported rousing scenes of Irish National Volunteers and Ulster Volunteers giving a hearty send off at Omagh to a draft of reservists for the Inniskillings.[12]

What if the 1916 rebels had succeeded – succeeded as they had envisaged it: a nationwide uprising, propelled by the guns on board the *Aud*, that then quickly evolved beyond the control of British forces leading to negotiated independence for Ireland? They might well have changed the course of the First World War. They might even have changed the course of world history. It is likely, for example, that there would have been no Battle of the Somme just two months after the Rising, simply because too many British forces would have been diverted from France. Ironically, the British might well have welcomed the diversion as they did not want to fight at the Somme (which had no strategic value) and were only doing so to appease their French allies then under pressure at Verdun. The Battle of the Somme might simply not have happened (along with the devastating losses suffered by the Royal Inniskilling Fusiliers on the opening day of the battle, one which saw my grandfather wounded – along with tens of thousands of others – and subsequently honourably discharged in 1919 after convalescence and service behind the lines in the Labour Corps).

As for changing the course of world history, consider what would have happened if a more successful Rising had indeed required a massive, military response from Britain. There is every likelihood that America would have stayed out of the war: Woodrow Wilson, the American president, was keen to enter the war on Britain's side, but had little, if any, popular support for doing so. What little support there was would almost certainly have evaporated in the face of Irish-America's reaction to what would have been Britain's inevitably harsh suppression of a nationwide Irish rebellion – a distraction Britain simply could not afford to prolong given the military threats it faced elsewhere. And if Wilson had stayed out of the First World War, then what? Such a counterfactual has already been imagined by economist and philosopher Hans-Hermann Hoppe:

> What would have happened, it is being asked again, if in accordance with his re-election promise, Woodrow Wilson had kept the US out of World War I? … If the United States had followed a strict non-interventionist foreign policy, it is likely that the intra-European conflict would have ended in late 1916 or early 1917 as the result of several peace initiatives, most notably by the Austrian Emperor Charles I. Moreover, the war would have been concluded with a mutually acceptable and face-saving compromise peace rather than the actual dictate. Consequently, Austria-Hungary, Germany and Russia would have remained traditional monarchies instead of being turned into short-lived democratic republics. With a Russian Czar and a German and Austrian Kaiser in place, it would have been almost impossible for the Bolsheviks to seize power in Russia, and in reaction to a growing communist threat in Western Europe, for the Fascists and National Socialists to do the same in Italy and Germany. Millions of victims of communism, national socialism, and World War II would have been saved. The extent of government interference with and control of the private economy in the United

States and in Western Europe would never have reached the heights seen today. And rather than Central and Eastern Europe (and consequently half of the globe) falling into communist hands and for more than forty years being plundered, devastated, and forcibly insulated from Western markets, all of Europe (and the entire globe) would have remained integrated economically (as in the nineteenth century) in a world-wide system of division of labor and cooperation. World living standards would have grown immensely higher than they actually have.[13]

If this hypothesis is accepted, not only would thousands of Irishmen (and millions of others) not have died over the next two and a half years of unprecedented slaughter as the First World War reached its brutish end, but the twentieth century as we know it would have been entirely different and far more peaceful. But while such counterfactual speculation is fascinating, it is of limited value as a guide to the future.[14]

Of course, in politics and the affairs of nations we know never to say never. Ireland's increasing involvement in peace-keeping and peace-making, as well as our obligations to other countries in the form of EU and UN treaties, will likely involve us in future conflicts, even as a neutral nation. However, it is unlikely our neutrality will survive the twenty-first century intact. The possible nature of violent threats that Ireland will face in the future – for example, an Islamic terrorist attack in retaliation for supporting the United States by making Shannon airport available – will require closer cooperation with police and military forces throughout the European Union in order to avoid such threats.

Indeed, one consequence of Ireland's peaceful success in recent decades may well be a growing expectation that Ireland will take greater responsibility for its own defence by way of involvement in Europe's defence arrangements, including NATO. George Orwell joked in 1945 that Irish nationalists were peculiarly blind to the reality that their proud independence was entirely due to the unspoken protection they enjoyed thanks to British military power.[15] Or as Thomas Paine put it more eloquently:

> Those who expect to reap the benefits of freedom, must, like men, undergo the fatigue of supporting it.[16]

In the 2016 Survey, we asked if people thought that by 2020 Ireland will no longer be a neutral country in military matters. Nearly one in four (23 percent) thought this likely to happen. However, only one in ten (11 percent) would like it if Ireland was no longer neutral.

In the Face of the World

Is it a uniquely Irish conceit to imagine that we can be a role model to other nations? We do have a number of unique attributes – we are an English-speaking former colony with very recent experience in violent strife and its eventual, peaceful resolution – which suggests we may have some lessons to teach others.

The 1916 Rising also made something of an impression on

other nations. Both Lenin and Trotsky welcomed it, though the former lamented that 'the misfortune of the Irish is that they have risen prematurely; when the European revolt of the proletariat has not yet matured'.[17] Even further afield, pan-African campaigners such as Marcus Garvey Jr, as well as the African National Congress, named their head offices 'Liberty Hall' (the headquarters of James Connolly's Irish Citizen Army) in recognition of the Irish rebels' legacy. Speaking at the formal dedication of the first such Liberty Hall as the Universal Negro Improvement Association's (UNIA) general meeting place in New York in July 1919, Garvey announced that:

> The time has come for the Negro race to offer up its martyrs upon the altar of liberty even as the Irish had given a long list from Robert Emmet to Roger Casement.[18]

But in a twenty-first-century world that is experiencing a global rebalancing from west to east, what possible role is there for Ireland as a role model for others? Of course, Ireland is already engaged directly with the world through trade and commerce. The Republic of Ireland's trade with China already greatly exceeds its trade with Northern Ireland: we import three times as much from the former as from the latter, and export twice as much to the former as to the latter.[19]

What do others think of us, in the face of the world? Consistently the number one driver of positive holiday experiences according to foreign visitors is the Irish people, followed by the scenery.[20] Beyond tourism we have the impact of the Irish abroad in general (including the Irish diaspora, as noted in Chapter 2), as well as the impact of certain well-known Irish personalities in particular, such as Bono and Bob Geldof. Such well-known figures have played a key role in raising global awareness about issues affecting developing countries, from debt to famine. They have also galvanised the generosity of Irish people to support charities at home and abroad. But we are far from being among the most generous people. One international study estimates that Irish charitable donations as a proportion of GDP (0.47 percent in 2006) are well behind those in the USA and UK (1.67 percent and 0.73 percent respectively).[21]

Having enjoyed our national freedom and sovereignty in peace since 1923 (in the Republic of Ireland anyway), the challenge of 2016 may well be to play a greater role in securing the same freedom and peace for others.

IDEAS FOR THE 2016 PROCLAMATION

Ireland is a lucky country – sometimes despite ourselves. We have left behind the ways of violence and have known peace for longer than most other countries in the world. The privileges and responsibilities that go with that – including the responsibility to protect what we have – will present us with new challenges as the twenty-first century unfolds.

Therefore our proclamation must look outward to the challenges and opportunities that Ireland's place in the world offers, and inspire this and future generations to play their part in leaving a legacy of peace, prosperity and freedom that will be a model to others.

6

Cherishing All
of the Children

*The Irish Republic is entitled to, and hereby claims, the allegiance
of every Irishman and Irishwoman. The Republic guarantees
religious and civil liberty, equal rights and equal opportunities to
all its citizens, and declares its resolve to pursue the happiness and
prosperity of the whole nation and all of its parts, cherishing all of
the children of the nation equally, and oblivious of the differences
carefully fostered by an alien government, which have divided a
minority from the majority in the past.*

WE HOLD THESE TRUTHS

The 1916 rebels consciously modelled their Proclamation on
those of previous rebellions – including the Fenians in 1867
and Robert Emmet in 1803. These in turn included elements
of previous declarations and proclamations, including – most
famously – the preamble to the United States' Declaration of
Independence in 1776:

> We hold these truths to be self-evident, that all men are created equal,
> that they are endowed by their Creator with certain unalienable rights,
> that among these are life, liberty and the pursuit of happiness.

In choosing similar words, the rebels were boldly stating that theirs was not simply a *putsch* or *coup d'état*, but rather that they were heralding a new beginning for Ireland and the Irish, one radically different from the past. With the benefit of nearly 100 years' hindsight, how successful were they in their stated ambitions for an Ireland that cherished all of its children equally?

Pursuing Happiness

The pursuit of happiness has rarely been to the fore in Irish political discourse – before or after independence – and yet it figures prominently in the ambitions of Irish rebels since the United Irishmen led by Wolfe Tone. Tone was responsible for circulating the *Secret Manifesto to the Friends of Ireland* in June 1791. Both Pearse and Connolly quoted the same sections of that manifesto in their writings before 1916, including these key parts:

> This society is likely to be a means the most powerful for the promotion of a great end. What end? *The Rights of Man in Ireland.* The greatest happiness of the greatest number in this island, the inherent and indefeasible claim of every free nation to rest in this nation – the will and the power to be happy to pursue the common weal as an individual pursues his private welfare, and to stand in insulated independence, an imperatorial people.
>
> The greatest happiness of the Greatest Number. On the rock of this principle let this society rest; by this let it judge and determine every political question, and whatever is necessary for this end let it

not be accounted hazardous, but rather our interest, our duty, our glory and our common religion. The Rights of Man are the Rights of God, and to vindicate the one is to maintain the other. We must be free in order to serve Him whose service is perfect freedom.[1]

This political idealisation of happiness came in turn from Thomas Paine, who, on observing the French Revolution in 1790 wrote in *Rights of Man* that 'whatever the form or constitution of government may be, it ought to have no other object than the general happiness'.[2] Tone and his co-authors of the *Secret Manifesto* were consciously referencing earlier texts much as the writers of the 1916 Proclamation would more than a century later.

The origin of the phrase 'the pursuit of happiness' in the seventeenth-century writings of John Locke suggests it was less an evocation of hedonism and more a harking back to the Ancient Greek concept of happiness called *eudaimonia*, or 'flourishing' as it is sometimes translated. Such a concept was explored in the philosophies of Socrates, Plato, Aristotle and Epicurus.[3] Wisely perhaps – in light of such philosophical challenges – Jefferson, Paine, Tone, Pearse and Connolly left 'happiness' undefined and therefore open to interpretation by their respective audiences and by future generations.

And yet, as we approach the centenary of the 1916 Proclamation, there appears to be an increasing interest in the politics and economics of happiness. A primary reason for this renewed interest is growing disaffection with more orthodox measures of a nation's well-being such as GDP. Though humanity has experienced unprecedented economic growth since the end of the Second World War, there is a growing body of evidence that increases in standard measures like GDP above a certain threshold have no bearing on some measures of people's happiness.

Of course, neither GDP nor happiness surveys were known in 1916, let alone in the times of Jefferson, Paine and Tone! The idea of measuring an economy in terms of the monetary value of its component parts was not developed until 1937 through the work of Simon Kuznets and other US economists. Furthermore, surveys of the general public's mood – whether in terms of happiness, quality of life or 'subjective well-being' as it is sometimes called – really only took off in the United States after 1946. Indeed, it was only in the 1970s that economists began to explore the link between GDP and happiness, inspired by the work of Richard Easterlin. He was responsible for identifying the 'Easterlin Paradox', i.e. the observation in some studies that there is no significant increase in a nation's happiness relative to others once a certain threshold of average income per person has been passed.[4]

In 2009, a report by the French government's Commission on the Measurement of Economic Performance and Social Progress challenged governments around to world to consider a wider measure of their people's well-being than just GDP:

> To define what well-being means, a multidimensional definition has to be used. Based on academic research and a number of concrete initiatives developed around the world, the Commission has

identified the following key dimensions that should be taken into account. At least in principle, these dimensions should be considered simultaneously:

i.   Material living standards (income, consumption and wealth);
ii.   Health;
iii.   Education;
iv.   Personal activities including work;
v.   Political voice and governance;
vi.   Social connections and relationships;
vii. Environment (present and future conditions);
viii. Insecurity, of an economic as well as a physical nature.[5]

Here in Ireland, the National Economic and Social Council (NESC) has also challenged the assumption that economic growth drives happiness or well-being (or that happiness and prosperity go readily hand-in-hand). They observe that:

GDP is a measure of economic activity and production in a country. Most people would accept that it is not a good measure of the well-being of an overall society or of the well-being of individuals within a society. There are two particular limitations of GDP as a measure of social welfare or social well-being. First, it is clearly a one-dimensional indicator, that ignores many dimensions that have long been recognised as essential, for example, children's education, health, affective relationships; and some that have more recently been recognised, for example, clean, safe and aesthetic environments. Second, it is an additive measure (national GDP is the sum of different incomes) and therefore ignores the many complexities in the relation between individual well-being and collective well-being. Hence, we require other measures of well-being …

A person's well-being relates to their physical, social and mental state. It requires that basic needs are met, that people have a sense of purpose, that they feel able to achieve important goals, to participate in society and to live the lives they value and have reason to value.

People's well-being is enhanced by conditions that include financial and personal security, meaningful and rewarding work, supportive personal relationships, strong and inclusive communities, good health, a healthy and attractive environment, and values of democracy and social justice.[6]

Again, we seem some way away from the original use of the word 'happiness' in the Proclamation let alone the American Declaration of Independence. But the question must be asked, nearly 100 years after a Rising meant to 'pursue the happiness ... of the whole nation', are the Irish happy? The answer is encouraging: despite being gripped by one of the severest recessions since the 1970s, recent surveys show that the Irish people are among the most satisfied with their lives in the European Union. In 2009, nearly nine in ten Irish people were very or fairly satisfied with the lives they led, versus fewer than eight in ten EU citizens as a whole (88 percent versus 77 percent). That is according to Eurobarometer, which has been tracking the opinions of EU citizens since the 1970s.[7]

Furthermore, the Irish appear to be among the happiest people in the world – as measured by life satisfaction, perceived quality of life or straightforward happiness – in a large number of comparative surveys. According to the World Database of Happiness, Ireland has enjoyed one of the strongest increases in life satisfaction since measurement began in 1973, and currently ranks in the top 15–17 nations for happiness and well-being.[8]

Moreover, Ireland's superior ranking in the happiness league (and in other, even more comprehensive indices such as National Accounts of Well-Being) has been accompanied by a huge increase in the country's standard of living (GDP again) since the 1960s.[9] In fact, by the ninetieth anniversary of the Easter Rising in 2006, Ireland's GDP per capita (simply dividing the size of the economy by the number of citizens, and adjusting for inflation and for currency fluctuations) was a staggering twenty-four times higher than it was at the time of the fiftieth anniversary in 1966.[10] Not surprisingly, and despite a recession, Ireland's GDP per capita (again adjusted for currency and price differences) stood at 43 percent above the average for all twenty-seven European Union member countries in 2008.[11]

Over a longer time scale, we can use measures such as the Human Development Index (HDI) to gauge the scale of improvement in Ireland's economic fortunes. Nick Crafts has estimated the value of HDI scores for a number of countries in 1913, including Ireland. The index is a composite of measures of per capita income, participation in education and life expectancy at birth. Back in 1913, Crafts estimated that Ireland's HDI score was 0.599, compared to 0.644 for the United Kingdom (excluding Ireland) and 0.711 for New Zealand. Ireland's HDI score in 1913 was higher than that for Belgium, Austria, Spain and Japan, among others.[12] By 2007, Ireland was ranked fifth in the world in terms of its HDI score of 0.965, with the UK in twenty-first place with a HDI score of 0.947. In 2007, the HDI scores for Cambodia and Congo were at the same levels as Ireland in 1913.[13]

It would appear then that the dual-aspiration of the 1916 Proclamation – 'to pursue the happiness *and* the prosperity of the whole nation' – has been substantially achieved as we approach the 2016 centenary, though not everyone would agree.

Unequal Opportunities

Constance Markievicz explained in 1913 that there were three great movements shaping Ireland: the national movement, the industrial movement and the women's movement, 'all fighting the same fight, for the extension of human liberty'.[14] We will turn to the women's movement in Chapter 7, but for now we need to consider the industrial movement and its importance for Ireland in the twenty-first century.

Markievicz was referring, of course, to the demands of trade unions and political representatives for better wages and working conditions for Irish workers. The Dublin Lockout of 1913–14 pitted tens of thousands of workers against several hundred employers in the bitterest labour dispute in Irish history. Its reverberations ultimately influenced the wording of the 1916 Proclamation.

Ireland – especially Dublin – was then gripped by horren-dous levels of poverty. It was estimated that nearly a quarter of children born in Dublin at the start of the twentieth century did not live to the age of one. As many as a third of all families in Dublin lived in one-room tenements in 1901, more than twice the level in London (and compared to just one percent of families in Belfast).[15] James Connolly reacted against such widespread misery by campaigning vociferously for a socialist Ireland. But he was not alone among the rebels in demanding a higher material standard of living for the Irish. Pearse too envisaged a free Ireland that would transform the living conditions of its people:

> A free Ireland would not, and could not, have hunger in her fertile vales and squalor in her cities. Ireland has resources to feed five times her population: a free Ireland would make those resources available. A free Ireland would drain the bogs, would harness the rivers, would plant the wastes, would nationalise the railways and waterways, would improve agriculture, would protect fisheries, would foster industries, would promote commerce, would diminish extravagant expenditure (as on needless judges and policemen), would beautify the cities, would educate the workers (and also the non-workers, who stand in direr need of it), would, in short, govern herself as no external power – nay, not even a government of angels and archangels – could govern her.[16]

But it would be wrong to portray Ireland as a whole as uniquely poor or exploited in a European context at the time of the Rising. As Joe Lee reminds us, referring to the conditions that existed upon the founding of the Irish Free State a few years later in 1922, Ireland in the early decades of the twentieth century was comparatively well off:

> The rulers of the Free State entered on the task of state building with many advantages. Ireland was already a relatively modernised society. Although comparisons of per capita income are notoriously difficult, Ireland's standard of living seems to have been about average for western Europe. It was, of course, only about two-thirds that of Britain. But the rest of Europe averaged only about two-thirds of Britain also …
>
> Educational attainment was generally higher, and more widely dispersed, geographically and socially, than in the new eastern European states. Irish literacy levels, verging on 100 percent, compared favourably with literacy rates of 70 percent in Bulgaria and Poland, 60 percent in Romania, 50 percent in Yugoslavia, and 20 percent in Albania.[17]

The tragedy, as Joe Lee narrates it, was not that Ireland had so little to begin with, but that other European nations with even less at the time managed to quickly and consistently pull ahead of Ireland on most economic and social measures over the rest of the twentieth century. Of course, Ireland eventually caught up on most measures, but the country was a (very) late developer in this and other regards.

Nevertheless, Ireland in the second decade of the twentieth century was characterised by considerable inequalities in wealth and income. The Proclamation's guarantee of 'equal opportunities to all its citizens' was testimony to the rebels' ambitions for social and economic reform, not just radical political change. That said, there is no agreed definition of inequality as such. But as an indication, one dataset has compared the share in national income of the bottom 50 percent of the population versus the top 5 percent in 1910 for various countries. The historical data for Ireland and Britain combined (they were one political entity at the time) saw the bottom 50 percent holding 19.4 percent of national income. This was fairly average for the time, though somewhat more than Russia and Turkey, and slightly less than France or Spain. On the other hand, the top 5 percent of the population in Ireland and Britain held 35.7 percent of the national income, again about average for the time. Fast forward to 1992 and the same calculations show an increase in the share held by the bottom 50 percent in Ireland and Britain to 24.2 percent; and a fall for the share of income held by top 5 percent of the population to 19.5 percent.[18] This still indicates significant inequality of course.

In more recent times, income inequality has continued to be a feature of Irish political debate and policy formation. One measure of income inequality is the 'Gini co-efficient' which looks at the distribution of income relative to the population. If everyone in a given population has the same income then the Gini co-efficient measures zero. If, on the other hand, only one person in a population has all the income and all the others have none then the co-efficient measures 100. Therefore the closer the measure is to zero the more equal the distribution of income in any given country.

In a contemporary international context, income inequality in Ireland is not especially severe. Ireland's Gini co-efficient in 2008 was 33, versus an EU average of 31: similar to that of the Netherlands and Finland. The country with the lowest co-efficient was Portugal at 23, whilst the highest was Cyprus at 38.[19]

Furthermore, the statistical evidence shows a modest but steady decline in income inequality in Ireland as measured by the Central Statistic Office's annual Survey of Income and Living Conditions (SILC). The SILC 2008 study reported not only a steady decline in income inequality since 2003 (again measured by the Gini co-efficient), but also an even more significant decline in the percentage of Ireland's population at risk of poverty. The latter fell from 19.7 percent in 2003 to just 14.4 percent in 2008.[20] Indeed, the same measure for other European Union countries shows that Ireland's poverty rate is now below the EU average and on a par with Germany and Belgium. Also, nearly 100 years after the 1916 Rising, Ireland's poverty rate is significantly below that in the United Kingdom.[21]

It would appear that on several key measures – such as income inequality and poverty – there is today some truth in the assertion that 'The Republic guarantees ... equal opportunities to all its citizens'. Although critics of Ireland's 'Celtic Tiger' experience would argue that the economic boom of the late 1990s and early 2000s was extremely unequal in the opportunities it offered, the data for inequality and poverty shows that things got better on several key measures for the Irish rather than worse. However, this still leaves the question of social mobility. Ireland throughout most of the twentieth century was characterised not only by poverty but by immobility: people born into a given social class rarely moved up (or down), such were the barriers to 'equality of opportunity'. This was a far cry indeed from the ambitions of the 1916 rebels, as articulated by Pearse:

No class in the nation has rights superior to those of any other class. No class in the nation is entitled to privileges beyond any other class except with the consent of the nation.[22]

Here again, however, the data suggests that some of the traditional barriers to social mobility in Ireland have broken down during the course of the long economic boom. Findings from a study by the Economic and Social Research Institute (ESRI), which surveyed trends in mobility between 1973 and 2000, found that:

Social mobility in the period 1973–2000 took place in the context of a significant upgrading of the class structure … In terms of absolute mobility, one of the striking consequences of such changes was increased access to the service class across the spectrum of class origins. Alongside such upward mobility we also observed significant flows from the propertied classes to the white-collar classes. The vast bulk of the change in social mobility patterns over time was accounted for by changes in absolute mobility, as Ireland converged towards a European norm from a traditionally low level of mobility. … contrary to the assumptions and predictions of many Irish sociologists, economic growth and, in particular, the economic boom of recent years has been associated with substantial social mobility and with increased equality of opportunity.[23]

However, the same authors caution that:

There is no evidence of a trend towards greater meritocracy. The advantages enjoyed by propertied groups in terms of social mobility are substantial and have remained undiminished over time. The association between class origins and education shows no sign of reduction … The most significant mediating role of education arises in relation to barriers to movement across the class hierarchy.

This highlights the crucial issue of education in relation to the ambitions of the 1916 Proclamation. Given Pearse's involvement in education this was inevitable, for as Joe Lee observed about Pearse:

… he has strong claims to be considered a major educational thinker, certainly by the standards of educational thought in the Ireland of his time, perhaps even by contemporary European standards.[24]

In his famous treatise on education – *The Murder Machine* – Pearse even proposed educational reform as the first task of a newly independent Ireland:

We can all foresee that the first task of a free Ireland must be destructive: that the lusty strokes of Gael and Gall, Ulster taking its manful part, will hew away and cast adrift the rotten and worm-eaten boards which support the grotesque fabric of the English education system. We can all see that, when an Irish government is constituted, there will be an Irish Minister of Education responsible to the Irish Parliament; that under him Irish education will be drawn into a homogeneous whole – an organic unity will replace a composite freak …[25]

As for a future Irish education system, he envisaged that:

In particular I would urge that the Irish school system of the future should give freedom – freedom to the individual school, freedom to the individual teacher, freedom as far as may be to the individual pupil. Without freedom, there can be no right growth; and education is properly the fostering of the right growth of a personality ...

The word freedom is no longer understood in Ireland. We have no experience of the thing, and we have almost lost our conception of the idea. So completely is this true that the very organisations which exist in Ireland to champion freedom show no disposition themselves to accord freedom: they challenge a great tyranny, but they erect their little tyrannies. 'Thou shalt not' is half the law of Ireland, and the other half is 'Thou must'.

Now, nowhere has the law of 'Thou shalt not' and 'Thou must' been so rigorous as in the schoolroom. Surely the first essential of healthy life there was freedom ... And I would promote this idea of freedom by the very organisation of the school itself, giving a certain autonomy not only to the school, but to the particular parts of the school: to the staff, of course, but also to the pupils, and, in a large school, to the various sub-divisions of the pupils. I do not plead for anarchy. I plead for freedom within the law, for liberty, not licence, for that true freedom which can exist only where there is discipline, which exists in fact because each, valuing his own freedom, respects also the freedom of others.

Pearse's ideas were undoubtedly radical for his time – and probably for our time too! He wrote approvingly about the Montessori educational system, and imagined an Irish system incorporating the best of Gaelic teaching traditions, including the inspiration of young minds with 'the hero-stories of the world, and especially of our own people'.

To this day, Irish people place a high value on education. One indicator is the proportion of the total population in primary, secondary and tertiary education combined in Ireland:

it is the highest in the European Union at 24.6 percent (the EU average is 19.0 percent).[26] A key factor driving such a high level of participation is the proportion of young people who remain in full-time education after they reach the age when schooling is no longer compulsory (sixteen years of age in Ireland's case and the norm in the majority of EU countries).

Here again the numbers are encouraging: Ireland belongs to that group of EU countries with very high levels of participation in further education beyond the compulsory school age. Some 85 percent of school leavers are still in full-time education in Ireland at age eighteen. This compares with just 50 percent in the United Kingdom and Germany.[27] As a result, by 2006, the number of Irish students in third level education stood some 30 percent higher than in 1998.

It is crucial that the expansion of educational opportunities as well as participation continues if the remaining barriers to social mobility are to become irrelevant. If that happens, then as we approach the centenary of the 1916 Rising we will be much closer to achieving the original goal of equal opportunities for all Irish citizens than ever before in the history of the state.

Alien Divisions

As we saw in Chapter 2, the Good Friday Agreement in 1998 heralded a new relationship between 'Gael and Gall' (to use Pearse's turn of phrase) on the island of Ireland. Nevertheless, it is a very different relationship to that envisaged by the authors of the 1916 Proclamation. When they spoke of 'cherishing all of the children of the nation equally' they were not referring to school children but to different traditions and aspirations evident in the tensions over Home Rule before the outbreak of the First World War. In particular, they were referring to unionists in the north of Ireland whom the rebels suspected of suffering from false consciousness due to 'differences carefully fostered by an alien government, which have divided a minority from the majority in the past'. It was not that simple, of course. Nor has it been since.

The original aspiration for a united, independent Ireland is still one that resonates with many Irish people. In the 2016 Survey, over half of all adults in the Republic of Ireland (54 percent) agreed with the statement: *On balance, it would be better for people on both sides of the border if there was a united Ireland.* Just one in six adults (17 percent) disagreed.

There were no gender differences in attitudes. Perhaps not surprisingly, two-thirds of those aged over 55 were in agreement (only 13 percent disagree). But even among 16–24-year-olds, nearly half (49 percent) agreed, whilst one in five (19 percent) disagreed. Curiously, agreement was lowest in Dublin (47 percent) and highest in Connaught and Ulster (outside Northern Ireland) at 59 percent. Again perhaps not that surprising.

But whilst a majority of people in the Republic of Ireland would like to see a united Ireland, few expect to see one. The 2016 Survey asked whether people expected there would be a united Ireland by 2020: fewer than one in ten (9 percent) thought there would, even though the majority (52 percent) said they would like to see a united Ireland by 2020 (especially older people).

The reality is that a united Ireland can only come about with the consent of the majority of people in Northern Ireland – as recognised in the Republic's new Articles 2 and 3 of its Constitution. As it is, some 44 percent of Northern Ireland's population is Catholic and 53 percent Protestant according to the 2001 Census. The next census will be in 2011 and will likely report an increase in the share of the Catholic population in Northern Ireland (not least because Northern Ireland continues to have the highest birth rate of any part of the British Isles and actually has a younger population than the Republic of Ireland).[28]

What if the 2011 Census reveals that Catholics comprise a slim majority share of Northern Ireland's population? The consequences would be interesting, to say the least. Certainly the majority of Catholics in Northern Ireland would vote in favour of a united Ireland in a referendum, according to opinion polls.[29] Of course these are just survey findings. Opinions, being opinions, vary all the time, and in the final analysis they don't cost anything to hold or to change. What does count are votes expressed in the ballot box: in elections as well as in referenda.

The protocol for deciding on a united Ireland is clear enough. Under the Northern Ireland Act 1998, the Northern Secretary may 'by order direct the holding of a poll ... if at any time it appears likely to him that a majority of those voting would express a wish that Northern Ireland should cease to be part of the United Kingdom and form part of a united Ireland'. A similar poll or referendum would have to take place simultaneously in the Republic of Ireland.

In the event that the 2011 Census revealed a Catholic majority in Northern Ireland, then the Northern Ireland secretary would certainly come under pressure to hold a referendum within a year or two of the results. Then, assuming a majority approved the reunification of Ireland in simultaneous referenda in Northern Ireland and in the Republic (as already noted, the Republic's constitution requires that a majority in both jurisdictions approve reunification), a few more years of procedural and legislative arranging could see a united Ireland by 2016.

A key question, of course, is whether the 2011 Census will show that a majority of Northern Ireland's population aged eighteen and over is Catholic? I suspect not: more recent data than the last NI census (in 2001), such as that on equality from NISRA, certainly indicates a near-majority of Catholics, but by no means an absolute majority. Another obvious question is whether all of Northern Ireland's Catholics would vote for a united Ireland. According to a recent opinion poll, the majority certainly would vote yes, but a large minority might well abstain or vote no.[30]

If there is a referendum on a united Ireland in the next few years then its advocates might note that the 1998 Act also requires that the Northern Ireland Secretary does not hold another poll for seven years after the previous one. Which means we might be looking at 2018–2019 for any sequel. In reality, few if any consider it likely that there will be a united Ireland any time soon. Even though it exists as an aspiration for many, in the course of practical planning and policy-making – in Dublin, London or Belfast – it simply does not figure.

No long-term projection or forecast – by the IDA, or any taskforce or any economist for that matter – assumes anything other than 'business as usual' for the next ten years in terms of the fundamental political and constitutional architecture on the island of Ireland. This is a reasonable enough stance as these things go: the future from the perspective of the present is uncertain enough without incorporating game-changing scenarios for which we have no precedent.

But of course it would be extremely naive to simply assume that a Catholic majority share of the Northern Ireland electorate would automatically translate into a demand for a referendum on a united Ireland, never mind a successful yes vote. As a prescient paper on Northern Ireland's long-term prospects – *A Long Peace* – observes, the Good Friday Agreement has created new challenges for nationalism and unionism alike, but especially the latter:

> Devolution, meanwhile, places significant responsibility for achieving success back into Northern Irish hands. This raises questions about whether the unionists have sufficient appetite to rise to these challenges. According to Henry MacDonald, 'The only way the Union will die in Northern Ireland is if the unionists kill it.' David Ervine, who leads the Progressive Unionist Party which is linked to the Ulster Volunteer Force, agrees. 'Unionism's own inadequacy could be its downfall,' he argues. 'That and refusing to believe in its own power and the legitimacy of its own arguments. We almost prefer to function with the siege mentality, allowing ourselves to be forced into a siege, rather than standing proudly and sensibly.'[31]

The authors go on to imagine how nationalists and unionists would 'set out their stall' to encourage progression towards – or movement away from – a united Ireland. First the nationalists:

It is fairly easy to predict how nationalists might start to build their case. They would invest considerable energy in developing political leaders who became widely recognised, however grudgingly, as effective, imaginative and fair. They would foster north–south ties, building not just cold and superficial formal links, but rich and dense cross-border networks, networks able to make a demonstrable contribution to Northern Ireland's quality of life. They would identify the enormous importance of boosting Catholic pride, self-reliance and self-confidence, by encouraging investment in education and enterprise, while actively seeking to draw in those otherwise at the margins. A successful community will gain momentum, their analysts would tell them, have high levels of engagement, and become used to winning arguments. It will also come out to vote. They would devote resources to research, analysis and communication, helping them listen to voters from both sides, understand their concerns, and tailor both policies and messages accordingly. They would adopt a tone that was increasingly confident; decreasingly strident and shrill. Finally, they would recognise the necessity of discipline, effective organisation and adequate resources. They would, after all, be embarking on a long journey, setting their sights on a distant goal.

The authors then imagine how unionists might appeal success-fully to Northern Ireland's electorate in this scenario:

Unionists could respond in kind – developing their own leaders, networks, and communities – and opening up a productive competition between two visions of the future. Alternatively, they could adopt a defensive, negative strategy, placing their hopes in cleverly proving that the case being built by nationalists was an illusion, a sham. Nationalist politicians only seem effective, imaginative and fair, they could argue. North–south networks are not all they are made out to be. Catholics might appear to be doing well, but this has been achieved not by fair means, but by foul. Voters should not be conned by the nationalist parties. Beneath the smooth nationalist exterior, something nasty lurks. Their discipline and organisation hark back to a paramilitary structure, and before that to a monolithic church. The bottom line: keep what you have, however imperfect, rather than risk seeking more.

Nevertheless, if the results of the 2011 census provoke a referendum on reunification – and a majority of voters on both sides of the border vote yes – then it is possible that we could have a united Ireland by Easter 2016, although I think this is a small possibility rather than a probability. However, I think it is far more probable that we could have a united Ireland by the centenary of the formation of Northern Ireland in June 2021 – an ironic coincidence indeed.

But crude population trends will not bring about a united Ireland on its own. The differences in attitudes and aspirations of peoples on both sides of the border are no longer 'fostered by an alien government' – indeed the government of the United Kingdom has made it clear on several occasions, formal and informal, that they would not prevent Northern Ireland seceding from the United Kingdom, if a majority voted openly and democratically to do so. Nor might such a scenario be confined to Northern Ireland – Scottish nationalists have also made some headway in recent years towards their ambitions for full independence.

Relations between the Republic of Ireland and the United Kingdom continue to 'normalise' in the face of shared challenges in the European Union and further afield. In the medium term, economic relations will be closer and more prosperous (especially if the UK joins the euro – admittedly a more remote prospect than Irish reunification). It was Michael Collins who wrote back in 1922:

> A prosperous Ireland will mean a united Ireland. With equitable taxation and flourishing trade our north-east countrymen will need no persuasion to come in and share in the healthy economic life of the country.[32]

So the future of Northern Ireland will be very much in the hands of its people. To the extent that the Republic of Ireland continues to succeed in its aspirations to 'pursue the happiness and prosperity of the whole nation and all of its parts' then the prospect of eventual unity with the Republic will be less daunting than it might have been in the past. However, that will never be enough on its own. Winning hearts and minds requires more than filling purses and wallets. Northern Ireland's own history is testimony to that.

IDEAS FOR THE 2016 PROCLAMATION

It has taken the best part of a century for relations between the north and south to become normalised alongside those between the Republic of Ireland and the United Kingdom.

The two countries now enjoy broadly similar levels of affluence, with Ireland having closed the very real gaps that existed at the start of the twentieth century.

Therefore our proclamation must look forward to a new era of peaceful economic convergence between these islands and the creation of conditions increasingly appealing to Northern Ireland's unionists to play their part in the shared pursuit of happiness and prosperity.

7

The Suffrages of All

Until our arms have brought the opportune moment for the establishment of a permanent National Government, representative of the whole people of Ireland and elected by the suffrages of all her men and women, the Provisional Government, hereby constituted, will administer the civil and military affairs of the Republic in trust for the people.

THE WHOLE PEOPLE

Not everything in the 1916 Proclamation was derived from previous declarations and proclamations. In 1916, advocating equality for men and women was a radical departure from the aspirations of those who, 'six times during the past three hundred years', had rebelled before. Three times in its brief text the Proclamation directly addresses men and women (or Irishmen and Irishwomen), signalling the commitment of the rebels (most of them anyway) to 'women's suffrage' as it was then known. Tom Clarke's wife Kathleen later revealed that one of the signatories (not her husband) was against equal opportunities for women – but she never revealed who.[1]

Feminists at the time recognised the uniqueness of the Proclamation's claims, including the Irish feminist Hanna Sheehy-Skeffington who, though not in favour of the Rising, and despite the murder of her husband Francis by the British forces engaged in the fight, nevertheless observed that:

> It is the only instance I know of in history where men fighting for freedom voluntarily included women.[2]

In 1916 only a tiny handful of countries – New Zealand, Denmark and Finland – allowed women to vote without restrictions. In a few other countries, women could vote in certain elections (e.g. local but not national), or if they were heads of household, land owners, taxpayers, or belonged to a certain race (e.g. white women but not aborigines in Australia at the time). Ireland, of course, was tied to the United Kingdom's legal position on women's suffrage. And inevitably, the rights of women in Ireland were bound up in the wider debate about Home Rule and independence. Indeed, a Conciliation Bill that would have given significant (though not universal) suffrage to women in Britain and Ireland was defeated on its second reading in March 1912, due to a tactical decision on the part of Irish MPs under John Redmond's direction to vote against it. Their rationale was that nothing should be allowed to detract from the more pressing issue of Home Rule for Ireland.[3] Of course, the outbreak of the First World War meant that both issues were sidelined until further notice.

The war did, however, transform the perceptions and experiences of women, which in turn drove renewed demands once the war was over:

> Yet, while the suffrage movement brought together nationalist and

unionist women (at least until 1912), and the nationalist and unionist movements each brought together women of all social classes, war work brought thousands of Irish women of all classes, religions *and* political affiliations together.[4]

Irish women (over the age of thirty and either a member or married to a member of the Local Government Register) were eventually given the vote – along with their sisters in Britain – as a result of the 1918 Representation of the People Act. Men over the age of twenty-one, regardless of property qualifications, were also given the vote – the rationale for the age differences was allegedly due to the smaller male electorate resulting from the huge loss of life in the recent war and fears of what a female majority might do! Subsequently, women in the Irish Free State were given full electoral equality with men in the 1922 Constitution, consciously reflecting the ambitions of the 1916 Proclamation. Indeed, Irish women achieved their 'guarantee of equal rights' six years before their counterparts in Northern Ireland and Great Britain, and many years before the majority of women around the world could vote.

BEYOND SUFFRAGE

One of the most significant social changes over the course of the past 100 years has been the profound shift in attitudes towards gender equality – of which women's suffrage was just one aspect. Though Ireland led much of the world in its enfranchisement of women, in several other regards Ireland was a laggard in providing 'equal rights and equal opportunities' to Irishwomen as well as to Irishmen.

Nevertheless, there has been a significant shift in attitudes in Ireland in recent decades, paralleling those evident elsewhere. This has been brought about by a sea change in women's involvement in the Irish labour market since the 1970s (especially following the abolition of the ban on public service jobs for married women). One example is the level of agreement with the statement that 'a man's job is to earn money, a woman's job is to look after the home and family'. In 1988, over half of all Irishmen (54 percent) agreed with that statement, compared to less than half of all Irishwomen (43 percent). By 2002, levels of agreement among men and women had fallen to 23 percent and 18 percent respectively.[5]

Not just attitudes but behaviour has also changed. In 1987 little more than a third (35 percent) of all Irishwomen of working age (15–64-year-olds) participated in the labour force.[6] Twelve years later, in 1999, for the first time the female participation rate exceeded 50 percent. By 2005, a majority of married women of working age were participating in the workforce for the first time. In 2009, despite the onset of recession in early 2008, the participation rate for all women stood at 54 percent (versus 71 percent for men).[7] The overall employment rate for Irishwomen is now the same as the average for all EU nations.

The Gender Gap

As we approach the centenary of the 1916 Proclamation, there is clear evidence of real progress towards the original aspiration of equal rights and opportunities for women and men in Ireland. But what gap remains in terms of completely realising that ambition – if any? And how big is Ireland's gender gap in relation to other countries?

The Global Gender Gap Index gives us some answers to both questions. The index examines the gap between men and women in four core categories, namely economic participation and opportunity; educational attainment; political empowerment; and health and survival.[8] The index benchmarks national gender gaps across the four categories and provides country rankings that allow for effective comparisons across regions and income groups, and over time. The rankings are designed to create greater awareness among a global audience of the challenges posed by gender gaps and the opportunities created by reducing them. The Global Gender Gap Report for 2009 contained detailed information on 134 countries (a list that has grown since it was first compiled in 2006). It therefore provides the ideal basis for comparing Ireland's efforts to provide equal rights and opportunities for women as well as men against those of other countries in the twenty-first century.

The first of the four categories – economic participation and opportunity – is captured through three concepts: the participation gap, the remuneration gap and the advancement gap. The participation gap is captured through the difference in labour force participation rates. The remuneration gap is captured through a ratio of female-to-male earned income and a survey on wage equality for similar work. The advancement of women and men is captured through the ratio of women to men among legislators, senior officials and managers, and the ratio of women to men among technical and professional workers.

The second category – educational attainment – is measured by the ratios of women to men in primary-, secondary- and tertiary-level education. Also included is the ratio of the female literacy rate to the male literacy rate.

The third category – political empowerment – is captured through the ratio of women to men in minister-level positions and the ratio of women to men in parliamentary positions. Also included is the ratio of women to men in terms of years in executive office (prime minister or president) in the last fifty years.

Finally the health and survival category uses the gap between women's and men's healthy life expectancy (in terms of the number of years that women and men can expect to live in good health), by taking into account the years lost to violence, disease, malnutrition or other relevant factors. A second variable included is the sex ratio at birth, specifically to capture the phenomenon of 'missing women' prevalent in many countries due to the widespread practice of sex-selection abortions.

On the basis of this comprehensive assessment, it is gratifying to note that Ireland ranks among those nations with the lowest gender gap in the world. Overall (combining scores from the four categories), Ireland ranked eighth among 134 countries surveyed in 2009 in terms of having the narrowest gap (Iceland ranked first). Ireland's ranking has actually improved from tenth place in 2006.[9]

Sub-rankings varied within the four categories, with Ireland ranking joint first in terms of educational attainment; eighth in terms of political empowerment; a much lower forty-third in terms of economic participation and opportunity; and a sharply lower eighty-sixth in terms of health and survival. The latter, rather unfairly, is driven by the low ratio of female-to-male births. This is unfair because Ireland happens to be extraordinarily successful at maintaining a low infant mortality rate due to the high standard of obstetric care which means that more boys survive at birth than would otherwise be the case. It is also worth adding that Ireland is the safest place in the world for a woman to give birth: Ireland's maternal mortality rate (the number of women who die during or shortly after giving birth per 100,000 live births) is the lowest in the world at 1 per 100,000. To put this in perspective, the global average is 400 per 100,000 and as high as a shocking 2,100 in Sierra Leone.[10] From a different perspective: Ireland's maternal mortality rate in 1950 was nearly 180 per 100,000 live births – similar to the present-day rates in Vietnam and Kyrgyzstan.

A FEMALE FUTURE?

Ireland is therefore a world leader in ensuring the equal rights of women and men as we approach the 2016 centenary. But there are some who claim we have much further to go – especially in relation to income inequality between men and women. A report in 2009, 'The Gender Wage Gap in Ireland', identified an overall wage gap (using 2003 data) that was almost 22 percent.[11] However, the report found that on average men have more years of work experience than women and that this is the single biggest contributor to this pay gap. Other factors – including a higher incidence of supervisory roles, longer tenure and higher trade union membership among men, and a higher incidence of part-time work among women – also explained some of the gap. Nevertheless, there is still a gap of 7.8 percent – or about one-third of the total – that could not be explained.

Not even this gap is (entirely) attributable to sex discrimination. The authors of the report recognise, for example, that women who have children may simply prefer to prioritise child rearing over career development as a matter of choice, with a knock-on impact on comparative wage levels. Other, countervailing factors may well close even this gap over time – for example, in 2004, for every 100 Irishmen graduating from university there were 130 Irishwomen, an increase from 110 in 1998.[12]

Moreover, a comparison of wages/salaries by age shows much lower gender differences among those in their twenties and working full time. The growing number of jobs demanding third level qualifications will inevitably be to the advantage of female employees. Ireland's increasingly credentialist society is therefore better suited to women than men in this regard. Indeed, the far more severe consequences of the recent recession for men (male job losses have been more than twice as high as female job losses), suggests we might see a more rapid disappearance of the remaining gender wage gap in Ireland than has been anticipated until now.

In the United States, some 80 percent of all job losses during the recent recession have also been among male employees. Hence some are calling it the 'mancession' because of such marked disparities. Men are losing jobs so quickly that women are expected to make up a majority of the US workforce in 2010 for the first time ever. Something similar is happening in Ireland: if the current rate of job losses by gender continues then men will become a minority in Ireland's workforce by 2012. Indeed, Ireland now has the largest gender gap in the European Union when it comes to its unemployment rate. In December 2009, the male unemployment rate in Ireland was 17 percent versus a female rate of 9 percent (the EU27 average was 10 percent and 9 percent respectively).[13]

The same EU data also showed another disturbing trend: youth unemployment in Ireland is among the highest in the European Union, with nearly a third (32 percent) of under-25-year-olds in Ireland unemployed. In January 2010, there were 86,000 young people on the Live Register in Ireland: 55,000 of these were young men.[14] One of the biggest economic and social challenges Ireland will face as a nation as we approach 2016 will be to ensure that a generation of young men in particular are not condemned to a lifetime of unemployment and under-employment as a result of the current economic crisis.

Taken to its logical extreme, such trends might see the emergence in Ireland of a 'she-conomy' by 2016, with women accounting for the majority of jobs and the greater share of consumer spending. As with all such extrapolation, however, it is dangerous to simply assume a continuation of the same trends inexorably into the future. Women are more likely to be employed in the public sector – including health, education and social services – which are crucially dependent on funding from the taxes raised from the private sector (where rather more men work). But as the latter continues to struggle its way back to recovery then public sector spending – including wage levels and numbers employed – will continue to come under pressure. This in turn will limit the economic power of women in the wider economy. As governments around the world struggle to get budgets back into balance as the recession gives way to recovery, it may well be women who lag behind men as sectors such as technology and energy (still predominantly male) lead a return to economic growth.

A further complicating factor in relation to such future projections is the massive increase in household debt during the economic boom. One consequence of the unprecedented and rapid increase in married women's participation in the workforce was the ability of households to borrow money. Instead of borrowing against one income, they could borrow against two. As a result many households will find that not only are the earnings of married women increasingly important to their standard of living, but that a growing share of those earnings will be consumed in repaying the debts built up during the economic boom.

Modern Families

Changing relations between the sexes in Ireland have not just been evident in the labour market. Indeed, some are beginning to wonder whether we have gone too far in terms of adopting and adapting to new social structures and mores in relation to gender. There are other forces at play – beyond the labour market – shaping gender equality in Ireland. The changing shape of family life in Ireland is just one indicator of the deeper changes under way.

As noted in Chapter 2, at the time of the fiftieth anniversary of the Easter Rising, the percentage of Irish births outside marriage stood at less than 3 percent. By the ninetieth anniversary in 2006 that figure had risen to 33 percent.[15] This is not just a function of lifestyle choices and shifts in cultural mores about pre-marital sex. It is also a consequence of deeper shifts in terms of economic independence for women and the substitution of the state (in the form of social welfare provision) for husbands for many mothers not in paid employment.

However, marriage in Ireland remains as popular as ever. In 1966, Ireland's marriage rate (the number of marriages per thousand population) stood at 5.2. By 2006 it stood at … 5.2.[16] The rate reached a peak of 7.5 in the early 1970s before plunging to 4.2 in the late 1990s. It subsequently recovered, peaking with the apex of economic growth in 2006–7. What is different about marrying couples nowadays is that the majority cohabit before they get married, in marked contrast to preceding decades. This partly reflects the preference of many couples to buy their own house before getting married, with the birth of their first children usually following within a year or two of the wedding.[17] So marriage is changing in Ireland (as elsewhere), but the one constant is its continuing popularity as a desired state for most young singles.

Gender relations have changed in Ireland in ways that were unimaginable to the writers of the 1916 Proclamation. It is unlikely, for example, that they gave much consideration – in terms of 'religious and civil liberty, equal rights and equal opportunities' – to gay rights. But just as women's suffrage appeared to be a fringe idea back in 1916, the same could be said for the issue of gay or same-sex marriage as we approach 2016. Of course, the latter issue affects far fewer people than the former. Women did and do make up the majority of the adult population after all; by contrast only 1.6 percent of Irishmen and 0.4 percent of Irishwomen are homosexual according to The Irish Study of Sexual Health and Relationships.[18] Moreover, it is likely that only a minority of Irish gay men or women (though more of the latter) will enter same-sex marriages. Perhaps as few as 2–3 percent if the experience of gay people in Sweden and the Netherlands – where same-sex marriages have been legal for some time – is anything to go by.

Curiously, despite the extraordinary strides made in relation to closing the gender gap, there is growing evidence that the increasing freedom of choice available to women in the developed world, including Ireland, has actually made women considerably less happy than men. Thirty years ago, it was the other way round: women repeatedly described themselves as much happier than men, but now men are happier than women.[19] Women are increasingly confronted with the 'Paradox of Choice', i.e. the finding that when we have more choices we also have another problem, namely that there are more things we cannot choose (where one choice by definition forecloses others). We become more conscious of the paths not taken. For Irishwomen and their counterparts in other developed countries in the twenty-first century, the paradox is that one cannot be both a career woman *and* a stay at home mother. Economists call it opportunity cost. Simply put, the true cost of something is what you give up to get it. That said, nobody wants to remove the freedom of choice brought about by increasing gender equality, even if it appears to make some people unhappy. Which suggests that we value freedom more than happiness, a trade-off the authors of the Proclamation were undoubtedly less familiar with than we are today.

In the 2016 Survey we asked whether people agreed or disagreed that *All things considered, I would prefer to live in Ireland than anywhere else?*

Nearly two in three Irish people (64 percent) agreed, 39 percent of them 'agreed strongly'. Disagreement was strongest among 16–24-year-olds and people living in Dublin.

Representative of the Whole People

One certainty that has remained since 1916 is that Ireland's true wealth lies in its people – women and men alike, as well as in our children. The nation's progress and success beyond 2016 will continue to demand the best contributions of all its citizens, which in turn will require that we avoid replacing the disadvantages historically experienced by women with a new set of disadvantages experienced by men. Or as Michael Collins put it many years ago:

> The real riches of the Irish nation will be the men and women of the Irish nation, the extent to which they are rich in body and mind and character ... But Irish men and women as private individuals must do their share to increase the prosperity of the country.[20]

Ideas for the 2016 Proclamation

Ireland has led the world in terms of women's rights and gender equality from 1916 to the present day. But the changes wrought in terms of economic, demographic and social outcomes have created new challenges for Irish society and for Ireland's future.

Therefore our Proclamation must continue to recognise the vital contribution of both Irishwomen and Irishmen to our country's success, whilst also seeing the process of economic recovery as an opportune moment to rethink our priorities and preferences in relation to work, family life and the institution of marriage.

8

August Destiny

We place the cause of the Irish Republic under the protection of the Most High God, Whose blessing we invoke upon our arms, and we pray that no one who serves that cause will dishonour it by cowardice, inhumanity, or rapine. In this supreme hour the Irish nation must, by its valour and discipline and by the readiness of its children to sacrifice themselves for the common good, prove itself worthy of the august destiny to which it is called.

THIS SUPREME HOUR

Do countries have destinies? Charles Stewart Parnell famously remarked that:

No man has a right to fix the boundary of the march of a nation. No man has a right to say 'Thus far shalt thou go, and no further'; and we have never attempted to fix the *ne plus ultra* to the progress of Ireland's nationhood, and we never shall. But, gentlemen, while we leave these things to time, circumstances, and the future … we shall not do anything to hinder or prevent better men who may come after us from gaining better things than those for which we now contend.[1]

He also observed in the same speech that 'it is given to none of us to forecast the future'. As we enter the second decade of the twenty-first century it might seem arcane – atavistic even

– to talk about the august destiny of a nation. People, especially politicians, just don't talk like that any more. And the history of most of the twentieth century taught us the dangers associated with 'the march of nations', especially by those indifferent to their neighbours' boundaries. So should we simply reject the notion of a nation's destiny lest it unleash something sinister, something fatal to the freedom we so cherish?

Others have considered these issues before. Writing at the end of the Second World War, the Austrian philosopher Karl Popper castigated those who believed that they had divined 'the meaning of history', which explained and justified all. In his view, such notions – especially the historicism of Hegel and Marx – were dangerous delusions. Instead, Popper concluded in his magnificent opus *The Open Society and Its Enemies*:

> … there can be no history of 'the past as it actually did happen'; there can only be historical interpretations, and none of them final; and every generation has a right to frame its own. But not only has it a right to frame its own interpretations, it also has a kind of obligation to do so; for there is indeed a pressing need to be answered. We want to know how our troubles are related to the past, and we want to see the line along which we may progress towards the solution of what we feel, and what we choose, to be our main tasks.[2]

His was not, however, a counsel of despair in the face of the task of historical interpretation:

> History has no meaning, I contend. But this contention does not imply that all we can do about it is to look aghast at the history of

political power, or that we must look on it as a cruel joke. For we can interpret it, with an eye to those problems of power politics whose solution we choose to attempt in our time. We can interpret the history of power politics from the point of view of our fight for the open society, for a rule of reason, for justice, freedom, equality, and for the control of international crime. Although history has no ends, we can impose these ends of ours upon it; and although history has no meaning, we can give it a meaning …

Neither nature nor history can tell us what we ought to do. Facts, whether those of nature or those of history, cannot make the decision for us, they cannot determine the ends we are going to choose. It is we who introduce purpose and meaning into nature and into history. Men are not equal; but we can decide to fight for equal rights. Human institutions such as the state are not rational, but we can decide to fight to make them more rational.

I interpret this as meaning 'destiny is not inevitable' – august or otherwise. To assume inevitability is to fall into the trap of historicism and all the risks (and evils) that it entails.

Ireland's destiny is what we make it – 'it is we who introduce purpose and meaning into … history'. And as we approach the centenary of the 1916 Rising, we have the opportunity to re-envisage – re-energise even – a shared sense of purpose and meaning that will enable Ireland to face a new set of challenges and opportunities in the twenty-first century.

AMÁRACH … AN DOMHAIN

One of the greatest challenges we face is globalisation. Ireland is one of the most open, most globalised countries in the world. Across many measures of trade, communications, financial flows and the movement of people, Ireland stands out relative to most other countries in the degree to which we are integrated into the world economy and global society. Is this our 'august destiny' as the new century unfolds? We inspired many other nations to secure their independence during the twentieth century; can we inspire other nations to embrace the extraordinary potential of globalisation in the twenty-first century, mindful of the risks it entails (as did independence)?

Globalisation – the deepening and widening network of economic and other flows between countries and continents – is the outstanding feature of the past thirty years and more. Not only has the world become more integrated, it has also become more interdependent. This in turn means that no nation is an island and that economic and political decisions in one country increasingly have a bearing on others. However, globalisation is not without its problems. Globalisation may mean growth for some, but it could mean falling wages for others in a race to the bottom. An absence of borders may be good for exports, but it also makes it easier for businesses to relocate to lower cost countries, costing jobs in the countries that they leave. We have seen both the positive and negative faces of globalisation here in Ireland, but for now the balance is undoubtedly positive.

There is no one single measure of globalisation, and therefore a phenomenon as complex and pervasive as globalisation deserves a comprehensive assessment. One such attempt at measurement is the KOF Globalisation Index.[3] This assesses the economic, social and political dimensions of globalisation across several key measures. As regards the economic dimensions, this component measures trends in variables such as trade and foreign direct investment. It also includes money transfers abroad by foreigners resident in a country to their home countries. Other more negative influences, such as tariffs and capital controls, are also included.

The KOF index also measures the social dimension of globalisation in terms of personal contacts (e.g. international telecom traffic and tourism); information flows (e.g. internet usage); and cultural proximity (e.g. domestic sales of foreign books and even the number of McDonalds restaurants and IKEA stores).

The final category of political globalisation is measured by the number of embassies and high commissions in a country and the number of international organisations of which the country is a member, as well as the number of UN peace missions a country has participated in. Also included is the number of treaties signed between two or more states since 1945 (as provided in the United Nations Treaties Collection).

The index shows that globalisation in the economic, social and political fields has been on the rise since the 1970s, receiving a particular boost after the end of the Cold War in the late 1980s and early 1990s. In the case of the KOF Globalisation Index for Ireland, our score has risen quite steadily from 65.2 in 1970 (the global average was 35) to 86.9 in 2007 (the global average was 57.5). Ireland ranked eleventh in the world in terms of the overall Globalisation Index (out of 208 countries surveyed) – ranking second in terms of economic globalisation, twenty-third in terms of social globalisation, and thirtieth in terms of political globalisation.

A different and more recent measure of globalisation for 2009 – The Ernst and Young Globalisation Index – places Ireland even higher in the rankings, at third in the world.[4] It also reported that Ireland was the country that has globalised fastest since 1995. As the authors observe:

> Smaller countries dominate the top of the Globalisation Index, measured by their integration in the global economy, because they generally rely more heavily on international markets for their growth and economic prosperity. Larger states, by contrast, are better able to fall back on their respective domestic markets. Unsurprisingly, the Index is headed by Singapore, which is highly dependent on international trade: aggregated imports and exports equate to over 300% of the city state's GDP ... Meanwhile, no G7 economy appears in the top 10: the UK sits at 15th and Germany at 16th, with the US at 24th. The two largest BRIC [Brazil, Russia, India and China] economies, China and India, appear 40th and 46th, respectively ...
>
> Ireland appears third overall in the Globalisation Index and has also seen the most significant improvement in globalisation of any country between 1995 and 2008 ... technology has been an important factor in this trend. In recent years, Ireland has positioned itself as a hub in the global exchange of technology, as a result of its safe operating environment and educated workforce. It may not be the originator of all the innovation that passes through its doors, but the country's role as a conduit for research and development (R&D) – through manufacture, packaging and export – has been an important contributor to its high level of globalisation.

Despite the global recession in 2008–10 (which particularly affected globalised economies like Singapore, Hong Kong and Ireland) the evidence from these and other studies shows that globalisation has driven Ireland's economic growth in recent decades at a rate that would not have been feasible otherwise. Indeed, Ireland's experience confirms that:

> … globalisation is good for growth. On average, countries that globalised more, experienced higher growth rates. This is especially true for actual economic integration and – in developed countries – the absence of restrictions on trade and capital. There is also evidence that cross border information flows promote growth. The accusation that poverty prevails because of globalisation is therefore not valid. To the contrary, those countries with the lowest growth rates are those who did not globalise.[5]

All this talk of globalisation may seem arid and bloodless, but we should not underestimate the extraordinary transformation Ireland – and the greater part of the world – has been through these past few decades. The poet Frederick Turner put it far more eloquently than any economist:

> In economics, we are recognising the exponential power of markets to generate wealth. Now that we have a global economy, the wealth of the average individual person on this planet doubles every twenty years or so, and our average life expectancy is now doubling every century … The world is not a zero-sum game, but rather a great cascade of gifts; if we lack for anything it is because of a lack of knowledge, not an unavailability of goods. Our problems are those of cash flow, scheduling, bottlenecks and distribution, so to speak,

not of the basic health of the balance sheet. We are threatened not by scarcity but glut. If we did not get in each others' way by bad and over-controlling governments and ideas, we would all be rich.[6]

Turner challenges the idea of the market as impersonal and cruel. He reminds us that the words 'market' and 'mercy' both come from the name of the Roman god of messengers and commerce, Mercury, as do 'commerce' and '.com' for that matter. Rather than something cold and cruel, the market is a place where we create value through our interactions with strangers, interactions that demand a level of trust and reciprocity in order for them to be sustained. And in creating value, we perceive ourselves as valued. The tragedy of the current crisis is that it results from a loss of trust and reciprocity (especially by the banks) that were and are essential to a healthy economy. Turner's is a very different take on the miracle of economic growth than we are usually subjected to in the writings of poets and artists (Irish or otherwise) it should be said.

And yet the 1916 Proclamation's signatories were not economists. They were political and union activists, teachers and lecturers, a shopkeeper, and part-time poets and writers. Their ambitions were not confined to economic gain and higher material standards of living for the people of Ireland, although they would have welcomed this. Rather, Ireland's august destiny – in their eyes – was something else: one based on a narrative linking our ancient history with present circumstances and future goals. I would contend that establishing a contemporary destiny demands a similar exercise in storytelling.

SCÉAL EILE

Though we face many challenges in Ireland, perhaps one of the most fundamental challenges we face is that of shaping a shared compelling narrative or story about our nation's future – and the path that will take us there. We once had such a story but we lost it. The story we told ourselves until recently went something like this:

> We are the young Europeans, with an ancient history behind us and an exciting future ahead of us. And our time has come to take our place on the stage of the modern world; to reap the benefits of modernity and to bequeath a much better country to our children and grandchildren.

I don't think this is the story we tell ourselves any more. Optimism, modernity and even the future have become tarnished by cynicism and despair brought on by the hyperbolic boom-bust we have experienced. But it will pass. And a new story will emerge and converge around new realities and possibilities. We have a long tradition of storytelling in Ireland, a tradition that will help us navigate a path to the future out of the difficulties we currently face. In his book *The Healing Power of Stories*, Daniel Taylor explores the connection between the way the human brain is 'wired' and our capacity for stories. He observes, for instance, that:

> … the human brain is so constructed that it actually processes experiences in narrative form. It seeks to integrate separate actions,

actors (characters), sequence, cause and effect (the primary link between actors and actions) into a meaningful whole …

Seeing our lives as stories, rather than as an unrelated series of random events, increases the possibility for having in our lives what we find in the best stories: significant, purposeful action. We all want very much for it to have mattered that we were here.[7]

This relates back to Popper's observation that 'it is we who introduce purpose into history'. For what else is history but a narrative about the past – a story told of choices made and paths not taken. But introducing purpose into a narrative about our nation – or any nation – and its future, requires the ability to imagine a variety of future stories, for stories multiply our possibilities. It is an act of imagination, which Taylor reminds us:

… links the past and present to the future, and gives us the possibility not only to know things, but to create whole new realities …

Stories engage both the heart and the head and move people to action. Statistics elicit counter-statistics and move people to argue. Stories demand a response (that is, responsibility); statistics encourage a rebuttal … The power of an imagined end, and it literally can only be imagined, lies in its ability to influence present choices.

The stories we tell ourselves about our future as a nation – and the choices that they inspire us to make – will do more to shape Ireland in five, ten or even fifty years time than anything else we do. And they will also tell us what kind of people we are … and will become.

In the 2016 Survey we asked people whether they expect that *Ireland in 2020 will be a better place than it is today, little changed or worse than today?*

Six in ten Irish people (59 percent) expect that Ireland will be a better place in 2020 than it is today. 16–24-year-olds are the most optimistic in that regard. Three in ten expect Ireland to be little changed. And only one in ten (12 percent) expect that Ireland will be worse in 2020 than it is today, especially those aged over 55 (though the majority of them still expect that it will be better).

We have chosen to use the vantage point of the coming centenary in 2016 to anticipate our near-term future. But what about the long-term future, say fifty to a hundred years out? How much technological, social and political change should we expect to see in Ireland in that timeframe? Given the vast differences – in all three realms – in Irish lives today compared to those in the early part of the last century, it seems beyond argument that enormous changes are in store the further ahead we look. Stephen Kinsella makes a similar point in *Ireland in 2050* – one of the few attempts made to take a long-term look ahead to Ireland's future. He notes that:

The Irish people can accommodate changes of breathtaking scale and scope to their daily lives, and those of their children and grandchildren …

Modern Irish life is conditioned around four to five-year political cycles, the yearly budget changes, and ten-year capital investment plans few people take very seriously at all, wrapped in the cycles the international economy goes through. While yearly budgets and ten-year plans are important, if fatally flawed documents, they do miss the really big picture, as we move from generation to generation to generation.[8]

And maybe that is why we need to tell stories: to help us better see and imagine the 'really big picture', and to be better prepared to deal with it when it comes, a task that should not be left to politicians, businessmen or economists alone. Daniel Taylor reminds us of another profound truth about stories: they are radical reminders of our freedom, because they insist on the link between character and plot, i.e. the choices we make – and their consequences – start with the values that we hold and personify.

> What is a character? A character is a bundle of values in action … Everything that happens in a story has the potential for revealing and forming character. The essence of plot is characters choosing. Like it or not, story tells us we are free and therefore responsible. We may be failures but we are not robots … Characters in stories must choose, and are responsible for the consequences of their choices. With choosing comes significance …
>
> By truly choosing, a character both limits freedom and gives it value. Each choice limits subsequent possibilities in a way that increases the likelihood of significance … Each choice in the middle reduces the possible endings, but without those choices the end would have no meaning.

The 1916 rebels understood character or 'values in action'. They spoke of valour, discipline and sacrifice, and, for the most part, they displayed character themselves in their behaviour. They also understood the consequences of choice, just as Pearse imagined in his poem 'The Fool':

> O wise men, riddle me this: what if the dream come true?
> What if the dream come true? and if millions unborn shall dwell
> In the house that I shaped in my heart, the noble house of my thought?[9]

The choices we make in the years ahead will be testimony indeed to the national character we – 'the millions unborn' – have inherited from those who have gone before.

EASTER ARISING

It has been remarked before that the staging of the Rising at Easter forged a powerful connection between the Easter story of sacrifice, death and resurrection and the actions of the rebels themselves. Pearse made the connection quite explicit: 'One man can free a people as one man redeemed the world.'[10]

Declan Kiberd recognises both the theatrical and the ecclesiastical elements of 1916, referring to Yeats' artistic response to the Rising thus:

> This was exactly the achievement of the 1916 rebels, who staged the Rising as street theatre and were justly celebrated in metaphors of drama by Yeats. All the mirrors for magistrates of ancient England had taught that 'to be fit to govern others we must be able to govern

ourselves': and the rebels had done just that. During Easter Week's performance, they were enabled both to show feelings and to control it: and so, in the eyes of their audience, both Irish and international, they had literally governed themselves. This ultimately invested them with a power far greater than their power to shock … The rebels' play was staged to gather an Irish audience and challenge an English one.[11]

And on the choice of Easter:

The selection of Easter Monday – when most British soldiers were on furlough at Fairyhouse races – was not just a sound tactic, but another brilliant symbolisation, since it reinforced Pearse's idea of the cyclical nature of history. Easter brought renewal, spring-time, new life to a dead landscape: and so it helped to justify and explain all previous abortive uprisings, for it wove them into a wider narrative, a myth of fall, death and glorious redemption.

Easter, traditionally, is about new beginnings: a re-enchantment, if you like, of life and the world we live in. Surely one of the greatest challenges humanity faces for this century is to find that path to re-enchantment that builds on our extraordinary achievements so far, and that avoids the pitfalls we are all too familiar with. But instead of enchantment, we have disillusion, caught as many are in the western world between philosophical nihilism and a narcissistic materialism. It doesn't have to be that way, and stories can lead us beyond the present trough of disillusion so many political and other leaders find themselves in.

The stories we tell ourselves of Ireland in 2016 and beyond

are the stories that will help us 'become the makers of our fate'. I believe the stories will be woven from three themes or storylines, namely: commerce, creativity and compassion. The first of these I have already addressed above: as one of the most globalised countries in the world, Irish businessmen and women can and will continue to demonstrate the remarkable capacity of Irish businesses engaging in free markets to create wealth and lift others out of poverty. Trade and commerce also makes friends of strangers – we are less likely to hate and kill people who have become our customers and suppliers. So material gain gives us freedom of choice and the peace to exercise it, but it does not guarantee wise choices.

Whilst an end to poverty is one critical step on the way to 're-enchanting the world', we also need creativity to channel the fruits of commerce. This is a task best suited to artists, which perhaps is why Oscar Wilde once predicted that 'the future is what artists are'.[12] Of course, at first glance his 'forecast' seems absurd. Yet the new insights of physics, evolution, astronomy and even psychology tell us we live in a world, indeed an entire universe, characterised not by scarcity and loss but by abundance and recuperation. It seems that life wants to happen – and to do so creatively.

Writer-artists like Frederick Turner anticipate a developmental shift in our cultural zeitgeist, enabled by the mature enjoyment of our material well-being. It is as if – as a society – we are progressing through the developmental stages famously defined by psychoanalyst Erik Erikson, emerging as a nation into what he called 'middle adulthood'. Erikson saw this stage as rich in potential for 'Generativity'.[13] With this term he referred to the motivation of middle-aged adults to seek satisfaction through productivity in career, family and civic interests: especially through concern for the next generation and the future. In other words, reaching maturity in the lives of adults – and perhaps of nations – can lead to a flourishing of creative output, productivity and the generation of content (artistic and otherwise) that we would not be capable of at younger ages. Erikson also saw this life stage as crucial because of the responsibility it places on each generation to prepare the next one for maturity – a duty of care.

Which brings us to the last of our storylines: compassion. The Irish are a compassionate people – as a consequence of our history, religious beliefs and the wider sense of our place in the world. As a globalised country we have benefited from the fruits of commerce, and we have even been able to 'punch above our weight' in terms of our creative outputs and their enjoyment outside of Ireland. But in relation to compassion, we have the opportunity to share with others the blessings we have enjoyed through our own hard work and good luck. Ireland has been here before, of course. The 1916 Rising and the turbulent times it bequeathed also coincided – some say inspired – the emergence of the Irish missions as a truly global force, one associated with the religious-inspired acts of self-sacrifice, hard work and generativity of those working in schools, hospitals and churches throughout the world.[14]

As we celebrate the centenary of the 1916 Rising, it will be incumbent on us to show that not only are we heirs to a dream of a free and better Ireland, but that we are willing to help others achieve the same dream. That would be a very fitting legacy indeed for the men and women of 1916.

IDEAS FOR THE 2016 PROCLAMATION

At the start of the twentieth century, Ireland demonstrated to the world the potential for small nations to shape their own destinies and to succeed in the face of hardship and hostility.

At the start of the twenty-first century, Ireland can again taking a leading role in demonstrating to all nations – large and small – the potential for commerce, creativity and compassion to transform the lives of billions; a fitting new chapter in our august destiny.

9

A Proclamation for 2016

Signed on Behalf of the Provisional Government,
Thomas J. Clarke,
Sean Mac Diarmada, Thomas MacDonagh,
P. H. Pearse, Eamonn Ceannt,
James Connolly, Joseph Plunkett.

ON WHOSE BEHALF?

One last finding from our *2016 Survey*. The question was:

> The 1916 Proclamation famously set out the ambitions of the rebels for Ireland after the Rising. In your own opinion, do you think that Ireland today is, on balance, a nation that they would be proud of, or one that they would be disappointed by?

Over six in ten Irish people (61 percent) say that they would be proud – just under four in ten (39 percent) say they would be disappointed. Younger people are more likely to feel that the rebels would be proud of Ireland today – older people are more likely to feel they would be disappointed (43 percent of over 55s). People in Dublin are more likely to feel they would be proud, those living in Connaught and Ulster (outside Northern Ireland) are more likely to feel they would be disappointed.

There are no differences between men and women in their opinions.

What does this tell us? The young, as ever, are full of hope and optimism – they also know no better, never having experienced the disappointment of unfulfilled dreams. The old are wiser, but also more prone to seeing the glass half empty – only too aware of what might have been and what will never be.

The average age of the signatories of the 1916 Proclamation was thirty-nine: Clarke was the eldest at fifty-nine, and Plunkett was the youngest at twenty-nine – more middle-aged than either youthful or elderly. And that, no doubt, was part of what drove them: the realisation that time was not on their side – neither politically nor biographically. But they did have some crucial advantages as middle-aged men: they still had some of the energy of youth, but had also gained some of the wisdom of age. As it happens, it was often middle-aged men who instigated change throughout history. Perhaps this has something to do with Erikson's idea of the generativity of middle adulthood: creativity and responsibility in a brief interlude of harmony.

Ireland's population in 2016 will be decidedly more middle-aged than it was in 1916, indeed than it has ever been. That raises an interesting prospect: will we witness a new flourishing of radical, innovative and alternative thinking in Ireland, driven by demography and catalysed by the centenary of 1916? Perhaps. But Erikson also warned us that there is a tension in every life stage, including middle-age. In the latter case it is the tension between generativity and stagnation. The latter is a possible consequence of middle-aged adults resting on their laurels, depleting the capital that they have accumulated, and taking 'least thought for tomorrow' or for the next generation.

THE 2016 PROCLAMATION

As I have written this book I have ended each chapter with some thoughts on the possible contents of a 2016 proclamation. Below I have gathered these thoughts together and written the words of a prospective 2016 Proclamation opposite the relevant section of the original proclamation: one I believe would befit the celebrations of the centenary a few short years from now.

The 1916 Proclamation	The 2016 Proclamation
POBLACHT NA H ÉIREANN	*POBLACHT NA H ÉIREANN*
THE PROVISIONAL GOVERNMENT OF THE IRISH REPUBLIC TO THE PEOPLE OF IRELAND	*THE FREE PEOPLE OF THE IRISH REPUBLIC TO IRISH PEOPLE THE WORLD OVER*
IRISHMEN AND IRISHWOMEN: In the name of God and of the dead generations from which she receives her old tradition of nationhood, Ireland, through us, summons her children to her flag and strikes for her freedom.	*IRISHMEN AND IRISHWOMEN: Drawing on our Christian values and the rich traditions bequeathed us by past generations, all of Ireland, through us, summons her children everywhere to celebrate our freedom and to join us in our new endeavours as a proud, independent nation.*

Having organised and trained her manhood through her secret revolutionary organisation, the Irish Republican Brotherhood, and through her open military organisations, the Irish Volunteers and the Irish Citizen Army, having patiently perfected her discipline, having resolutely waited for the right moment to reveal itself, she now seizes that moment, and, supported by her exiled children in America and by gallant allies in Europe, but relying in the first on her own strength, she strikes in full confidence of victory.	*Having founded and fashioned a young nation from an old people, in the face of fear and adversity, but always with hope and determination, we now seize this moment. Nourished by the energy and discipline of the organisations and institutions we have shaped as a free people, supported by the friendship of Irish descendants throughout the world, and by our fellow citizens in the European Union, but relying first on our own strength, we now confidently stride forward to our nation's future.*
We declare the right of the people of Ireland to the ownership of Ireland, and to the unfettered control of Irish destinies, to be sovereign and indefeasible. The long usurpation of that right by a foreign people and government has not extinguished the right, nor can it ever be extinguished except by the destruction of the Irish people.	*We declare the right of the people of Ireland to be the final arbiters in how we govern ourselves, founded on democratic principles, to be sovereign and indefeasible. That right includes the voluntary sharing of sovereignty with other peoples in order that our nation can endeavour with others to face common challenges, as necessary, to ensure a better future for the Irish people.*

In every generation the Irish people have asserted their right to national freedom and sovereignty; six times during the last three hundred years they have asserted it in arms. Standing on that fundamental right and again asserting it in arms in the face of the world, we hereby proclaim the Irish Republic as a Sovereign Independent State, and we pledge our lives and the lives of our comrades-in-arms to the cause of its freedom, of its welfare, and of its exaltation among the nations.

Ours is a fortunate generation of Irish people, one of only a few to have lived in a free and sovereign nation. Through the labour and vision of past generations, we now enjoy the rights that they asserted. Mindful of this inheritance, and also of the responsibility that every generation has to protect and pass on our freedom to the next generation, we hereby proudly re-proclaim the Irish Republic as a Sovereign Independent State. We pledge, through the lives we lead, to warrant the faith put in us by past generations and to ensure Ireland's esteem among the free nations of the world.

The Irish Republic is entitled to, and hereby claims, the allegiance of every Irishman and Irishwoman. The Republic guarantees religious and civil liberty, equal rights and equal opportunities to all its citizens, and declares its resolve to pursue the happiness and prosperity of the whole nation and all of its parts, cherishing all of the children of the nation equally and oblivious of the differences carefully fostered by an alien government, which have divided a minority from the majority in the past.

The perpetuation of the Irish Republic requires the allegiance of every Irishman and Irishwoman. As a peaceful and democratic nation, the Republic guarantees religious and civil liberty, equal rights and equal opportunities to all its citizens, especially to our children, and declares its resolve to pursue the happiness and prosperity of the whole nation and all its parts. It is the firm will of the Irish nation, in harmony and friendship, to unite all the people of different traditions on the island of Ireland in a united Ireland, with the consent of a majority in both jurisdictions of the island.

Until our arms have brought the opportune moment for the establishment of a permanent National Government representative of the whole people of Ireland and elected by the suffrages of all her men and women, the Provisional Government, hereby constituted, will administer the civil and military affairs of the Republic in trust for the people.

Ireland has led the world in its demands for equal rights for all men and women in the cause of its freedom. We can be proud of our achievements in enabling Irishwomen and Irishmen to play their full part in a flourishing Republic. Now is the opportune moment to use our peace, prosperity and freedom to respond imaginatively to the challenges of economic, social and family change that we face in Ireland, and in doing so to be an inspiration to others.

We place the cause of the Irish Republic under the protection of the Most High God, Whose blessing we invoke upon our arms, and we pray that no one who serves that cause will dishonour it by cowardice, inhumanity, or rapine. In this supreme hour the Irish nation must, by its valour and discipline and by the readiness of its children to sacrifice themselves for the common good, prove itself worthy of the august destiny to which it is called.

The Irish people are justly proud of our achievements as a sovereign, independent nation. In the domains of commerce, creativity and compassion, we continue to demonstrate our capacity for bravery, humanity and sacrifice, as well as our enthusiastic engagement with the wider world. But each generation faces new trials, and ours is no exception. In this supreme hour, the Irish nation must forge a common purpose that will guide us through the difficult times ahead. By so doing, we will once again prove ourselves worthy of the august destiny to which we are called.

Signed on Behalf of the Provisional Government, *Thomas J. Clarke, Sean Mac Diarmada, Thomas MacDonagh, P. H. Pearse, Eamonn Ceannt, James Connolly, Joseph Plunkett.*	*Signed on behalf of the free people of the Irish Republic.*

WILL YOU SIGN IT?

Of course, these are just my words. I do not presume to speak on behalf of the Irish people. But if you have been inspired by this book to think again about the 1916 Rising, the Proclamation and its relevance to you today and tomorrow, then tell me what you think.

Join me and others at *The 2016 Proclamation* website – www.the2016proclamation.ie – and share your thoughts on the issues and ideas raised in this book. And take your turn at drafting *The 2016 Proclamation*. Let us do this together.

Ní neart go cur le chéile …

The 2016 Proclamation

POBLACHT NA H EIREANN.

THE FREE PEOPLE

OF THE

IRISH REPUBLIC

TO IRISH PEOPLE THE WORLD OVER

IRISHMEN AND IRISHWOMEN: Drawing on our Christian values and the rich traditions bequeathed us by past generations, all of Ireland, through us, summons her children everywhere to celebrate our freedom and to join us in our new endeavours as a proud, independent nation.

Having founded and fashioned a young nation from an old people, in the face of fear and adversity, but always with hope and determination, we now seize this moment. Nourished by the energy and discipline of the organisations and institutions we have shaped as a free people, supported by the love of Irish descendants throughout the world, and by our fellow citizens in the European Union, but relying first on our own strength, we now confidently stride forward to our nation's future.

We declare the right of the people of Ireland to be the final arbiters in how we govern ourselves, founded on democratic principles, to be sovereign and indefeasible. That right includes the voluntary sharing of sovereignty with other peoples in order that our nation can endeavour with other nations to face common challenges as necessary to ensure a better future for the Irish people.

Ours is a fortunate generation of Irish people, one of only a few to have lived in a free and sovereign nation. Through the labour and vision of past generations, we now enjoy the rights that they asserted. Mindful of this inheritance, and also of the responsibility that every generation has to protect and pass on our freedom to the next generation, we hereby proudly re-proclaim the Irish Republic as a Sovereign Independent State. We pledge, through the lives we lead, to warrant the faith put in us by past generations and to ensure Ireland's esteem among the free nations of the world.

The perpetuation of the Irish Republic necessitates the allegiance of every Irishman and Irishwoman. As a peaceful and democratic nation, the Republic guarantees religious and civil liberty, equal rights and equal opportunities to all its citizens, and declares its resolve to pursue the happiness and prosperity of the whole nation and all its parts. It is the firm will of the Irish nation, in harmony and friendship, to unite all the people of different traditions on the island of Ireland in a united Ireland, with the consent of a majority in both jurisdictions in the island.

Ireland led the world in its demands for equal rights for all men and women in the cause of its freedom. Ireland can be proud of its achievements in enabling Irishwomen and Irishmen to play their full part in a flourishing Republic. Now is the opportune moment to use our peace, prosperity and freedom to respond imaginatively to the new challenges of social and family change in Ireland.

The Irish people are justly proud of our achievements as a sovereign, independent nation. In the domains of commerce, creativity and compassion, we continue to demonstrate our capacity for bravery, humanity and sacrifice. But each generation faces new trials, and ours is no exception. In this supreme hour, the Irish nation must forge a common purpose that will guide us through the difficult times ahead. By so doing, we will once again prove ourselves worthy of the august destiny to which we are called.

Signed on behalf of the free people of the Irish Republic,

Notes

INTRODUCTION

1   The 2016 Survey was a nationally representative survey of 1,000 adults aged sixteen to seventy-five conducted by Amárach Research in January 2010 for this book. The sample comprised 850 online interviews and 150 face-to-face interviews, with non-interlocking sampling quotas for age, gender and social class.

1   THE PEOPLE OF IRELAND

1   The definitive guide to the writing of the proclamation is John O'Connor, *The 1916 Proclamation* (Anvil Books, 1999).

2   Iarfhlaith Watson, Máire Nic Ghiolla Phádraig, Fiachra Kennedy and Bernadette Rock-Huspatel, 'National Identity and Anti-Immigrant Attitudes', in Betty Hilliard and Máire Nic Ghiolla Phádraig (eds), *Changing Ireland in International Comparison* (The Liffey Press, 2007), pp. 217–242. See pp. 222–23.

3   *Ibid.,* p. 232.

4   *Ibid.,* p. 241.

5   Richard English, *Irish Freedom: The History of Nationalism in Ireland* (Macmillan, 2006), pp. 435, 444.

6   Eldad Davidov, 'Measurement equivalence of nationalism and constructive patriotism in the ISSP 2003: 34 countries in a comparative perspective', *Political Analysis* 17 (1), January 2009, pp. 64–82. See p. 64.

7   Tom W. Smith and Seokho Kim, *National Pride in Comparative Perspective: 1995–96 and 2003–04*, NORC/University of Chicago, GSS Cross-national Report No. 26, November 2005.

8   See for example, the Lisbon Treaty Post-Referendum Survey, Ireland 2009, Eurobarometer Report No. 284, October 2009.
9   Details and discussions are reported on the event's website: www. globalirishforum.ie.
10 'Ireland and the Irish Abroad', Department of Foreign Affairs, launched in December 2001 by the then Minister for Foreign Affairs, Brian Cowen, TD.
11 Quarterly National Household Survey, Q2 2009, Table A1, Central Statistics Office (CSO). The best place to access CSO information is on their website: www.cso.ie.
12 Clair Wills, *Dublin 1916 – The Siege of the GPO* (Profile Books, 2009), p. 12.
13 Marc Coleman, *The Best is Yet to Come* (Blackhall Publishing, 2007), pp. 127–29.
14 Dan O'Brien, *Ireland, Europe and the World* (Gill & Macmillan, 2009), pp. 3–4.
15 See the findings from the Flash Eurobarometer Reports on Post-Referendum Surveys in Ireland, 245 and 284, 2008–09.
16 For a brilliant exposition of the unique strengths of Europe and the European Union see Mark Leonard, *Why Europe Will Run the Twenty-First Century* (Fourth Estate Ltd, 2005).

2   THE DEAD GENERATIONS

1   Garret FitzGerald, 'Rising and early independence brought prosperity', *Irish Times*, 12 April 2006.
2   Details of all Nobel Prize winners are available on the NobelPrize.org website.
3   Figures from www.gaelscoileanna.ie website.
4   Data from the CSO Census 2006 Report: Volume 13 – Religion.
5   Ronan Fanning, 'The age of our craven deference is finally over', *Sunday Independent*, 6 December 2009.

6   The WVS website – www.worldvaluessurvey.com – is an excellent
    resource enabling users to create their own tables from surveys covering
    a range of topics in many countries over several years.

7   Research reported by the Iona Institute in November 2009, available
    at: www.ionainstitute.ie.

8   Dr Micheál MacGreil, SJ, *The Challenge of Indifference* (Veritas, 2009).

9   Reported in CSO Vital Statistics series.

10 Data from Table 5, 'Population statistics in Europe 2008: first results',
    Eurostat, Issue 31, 2009, pp. 1–11.

11 See pewglobal.org/reports/pdf/262.pdf, p. 20.

12 Tom Garvin, *Preventing the Future: Why was Ireland so poor for so long?*
    (Gill & Macmillan, 2004).

13 *Ibid.*, p. 202.

14 *Ibid.*, p. 212.

15 Tearfund, 'Churchgoing in the UK', www.tearfund.org, 2007.

16 Richard Koch & Chris Smith, *Suicide of the West* (Continuum
    International Publishing Group, 2006).

17 Deepak Lal, 'Reviving the Invisible Hand: the case for classical
    liberalism in the twenty-first century', RSA lecture, June 2008.

18 Taken from the IDA's famous marketing campaign in the 1980s which
    emphasised Ireland's youthful workforce as one of the key strengths to
    attract overseas investors.

19 John Kay, 'The Future of Markets', 20 October 2009, http://www.
    wincott.co.uk/lecture2009.htm.

20 Available from www.heritage.org/Index.

21 Fraser Institute, www.freetheworld.com/release.html, September 2009.

22 Niall Ferguson, 'Sinking Globalisation', *Foreign Affairs*, March/April
    2005, pp. 64–77.

3   Now Seizes that Moment

1   Charles Townshend, *Easter 1916 – The Irish Rebellion* (Penguin, 2006).

See Chapter 2, 'The Militarisation of Politics'.

2   'Community Involvement and Social Networks in Ireland 2006', CSO, 2009.

3   Quarterly National Household Survey – Union Membership Q2 2007, CSO, April 2008.

4   Robert D. Putnam, 'E Pluribus Unum: Diversity and Community in the Twenty-First Century', *Scandinavian Political Studies*, Volume 30, Issue 2, pp. 137–74.

5   Standard Eurobarometer 70, December 2008, published by the European Commission.

6   'Discrimination in the European Union: Perceptions, Experiences and Attitudes', Eurobarometer ref. 296, July 2008.

7   Presentation to the National Integration Debate, 10 September 2008, on www.amarachresearch.blogspot.com.

8   *Ibid.*

9   David Goodhart, 'The baby-boomers finally see sense on immigration', *The Observer*, 24 February 2008.

10 Described in Mick O'Farrell, *50 Things You Didn't Know About 1916* (Mercier Press, 2009), p. 54.

11 James Ogilvy, 'Earth Might Be Fair', in Sheila Moorcroft (ed.), *Visions for the 21st Century* (Praeger, 1993), pp. 148–178.

12 From www.Internetworldstats.com/stats7.htm.

13 Johnny Ryan, *Countering Militant Islamist Radicalisation on the Internet: a User Driven Strategy to Recover the Web* (Institute of International and European Affairs, 2007).

14 *Ibid.*, p. 8.

15 Clive Thompson, 'Brave New World of Digital Intimacy', *The New York Times*, 5 September 2008.

16 Clay Shirky, *Here Comes Everybody: The Power of Organizing Without Organizations* (Penguin, 2008).

17 Proceedings and background details available at www.globalirishforum. ie. The Innovation Fund Ireland – announced by the Taoiseach in July

2010 – is one example of the fruits of the Farmleigh initiative (though it is early days yet as to its impact).

18 'Skills in Creativity, Design and Innovation', Forfás, November 2009.

19 'Your Country Needs Innovative Minds!', Deutsche Bank Research, November 2009.

20 Definition from en.wikipedia.org/wiki/Kairos.

4   THE RIGHT OF THE PEOPLE

1 See relevant chapters in *The Statistical Yearbook of Ireland 2009*, published by the Central Statistics Office.

2 Census 1946 Volume 4 – Housing and Social Amenities, Part II – Table 12 in CSO Census Archive: http://www.cso.ie/Census/ historical_reports.htm.

3 See Eurostat data: epp.eurostat.ec.europa.eu/statistics_explained/ index.php/Housing_statistics.

4 See Table 19, Census 2006, Volume 6 – Housing, Central Statistics Office (CSO).

5 See 'Chapter 1: 1900–1912' in Diarmaid Ferriter, *The Transformation of Ireland* (Overlook Press, 2007).

6 From *Workers' Republic*, 24 September 1898 (part of an excellent archive of Connolly's writings: www.marxists.org/archive/connolly/ index.htm).

7 'The Sovereign People', March 1916, in *Collected Works of Pádraic H. Pearse – Political Writings and Speeches* (Maunsel & Roberts Ltd, 1922). Available as a free download: www.archive.org/details/ cu31924028175259.

8 *Bunreacht na hÉireann – Constitution of Ireland, 1937* (full text and details of amendments: www.taoiseach.gov.ie/attached_files/html files/Constitution of Ireland(Eng)Nov2004.htm.

9 The Committee's reports are available at www.constitution.ie.

10 'Index of Economic Freedom', 2009, The Heritage Foundation: www. heritage.org/Index/Country/Ireland.

11 *Ibid.*

12 Daniel Bell, 'The World and the United States in 2013', *Daedalus* 116 (3), 1987, pp. 1–33.

13 Immanuel Wallerstein, 'States? Sovereignty? The Dilemmas of Capitalists in an age of Transition', (1996): fbc.binghamton.edu/ iwsovty.htm.

14 Speech by Eamon de Valera at the League of Nations, September 1935, in Michael McLoughlin, *Great Irish Speeches of the Twentieth Century* (Poolbeg, 1996), pp. 173–4.

15 Speech by the Taoiseach, Mr Brian Cowen, TD, 90th Anniversary of Dáil Éireann, Tuesday, 20 January 2009 (www.taoiseach.gov.ie).

16 Standard Eurobarometer 72, 'First Results, Fieldwork: October to November 2009', published online by the European Commission, December 2009, http://ec.europa.eu/public_opinion/archives/eb/ eb72/eb72_en.htm

17 Kurt Taylor Gaubatz, 'City-State Redux: Rethinking Optimal State Size in an Age of Globalization', *New Global Studies*, Vol. 3, Issue 1, Article 1, 2009, pp. 1–23.

18 Full text of Treaty: eurlex.europa.eu/en/treaties/dat/11992M/htm/ 11992M.html.

19 The Futures Academy, Dublin Institute of Technology, March 2008: www.thefuturesacademy.ie/publications/reports-papers.

5   EXALTATION AMONG THE NATIONS

1 Catriona Pennell, 'Going to War', in John Horne (ed.), *Our War: Ireland and the Great War* (Royal Irish Academy, 2008), pp. 35–48.

2 An Addendum to *How Does She Stand?* by Pádraic Pearse (August 1914), www.ucc.ie/celt/published/E900007-002.

3 James Connolly, 'The National Danger', *Irish Worker*, 15 August 1914.

4   'Peace and the Gael', December 1915, in *Collected Works of Pádraic H. Pearse – Political Writings and Speeches* (Maunsel & Roberts Ltd, 1922). Available to download: www.archive.org/details/cu31924028175259.

5   George Orwell, *Notes on Nationalism*, May 1945; see archive of political writings of George Orwell: www.resort.com/~prime8/Orwell/.

6   For a contrarian perspective – that democracy ultimately undermines nations and nationalities – see Hans-Hermann Hoppe, *Democracy, the God that Failed* (Transaction Publishers, 2001); more at: www.hanshoppe.com/publications.

7   The Global Peace Index 2009, Institute for Economics & Peace: www.visionofhumanity.org/gpi/home.php.

8   'Peace: its Causes and Economic Value', 2009 Discussion Paper, Institute for Economics & Peace; www.visionofhumanity.org/gpi/documents/discussion-papers.php.

9   'Human Development Report 2009', United Nations Development Programme (UNDP): hdrstats.undp.org/en/countries/country_fact_sheets/cty_fs_IRL.html.

10 Stephen Pinker, 'Why is there Peace?', *Greater Good Magazine*, April 2009: http://greatergood.berkeley.edu/article/item/why_is_there_peace.

11 Dave Duggan's, *Still, the Blackbird Sings*, a play about the poet Francis Ledwidge who joined the Inniskillings, captures this tension brilliantly.

12 W.J. Canning, *A Wheen of Medals, The History of the 9th (Service) Bn of the Royal Inniskilling Fusiliers (The Tyrones) in World War One* (self-published, 2006).

13 'Introduction' in Hans-Hermann Hoppe, *Democracy, the God that Failed* (Transaction Publishers, 2001)

14 For a contrasting counterfactual see 'What if there had been no 1916 Rising?' in Diarmaid Ferriter, *What If? Alternative Views of Twentieth-Century Ireland* (Gill & Macmillan, 2006).

15 George Orwell, *Notes on Nationalism*, May 1945; see archive of political

writings of George Orwell: www.resort.com/~prime8/Orwell/.

16 Thomas Paine, *The American Crisis* (1776).

17 Cited in Mick O'Farrell, *50 Things You Didn't Know About 1916* (Mercier Press, 2009) p. 110.

18 From the introduction in Robert A. Hill (ed.), *The Marcus Garvey & UNIA Papers*, Volume 2 (University of California Press, 1983).

19 'External Trade September 2009', CSO Bulletin, December 2009.

20 See the annual visitor surveys conducted by Fáilte Ireland: http://www. failteireland.ie/Research---Statistics/Surveys-and-Reports/Visitor-Attitudes-Survey.

21 'International comparisons of charitable giving', CAF briefing paper, Charities Aid Foundation, November 2006.

6   CHERISHING ALL OF THE CHILDREN

1 Quoted by Pádraic Pearse in *The Separatist Ideal*, February 1916 in *Collected Works of Pádraic H. Pearse – Political Writings and Speeches* (Maunsel & Roberts Ltd, 1922); and by James Connolly in Chapter 8 of *Labour in Irish History* (1910), p. 90, www.ucc.ie/celt/published/ E900002-001.

2 Thomas Paine, *Rights of Man: Being an Answer to Mr Burke's Attack on the French Revolution* (1790), p. 145.

3 Carol V. Hamilton, 'The Surprising Origins and Meaning of the "Pursuit of Happiness"', *History Network News*, January 2007, http:// hnn.us/articles/46460.html.

4 Richard Easterlin, 'Does Economic Growth Improve the Human Lot?' in Paul A. David and Melvin W. Reder (eds), *Nations and Households in Economic Growth: Essays in Honor of Moses Abramovitz* (New York: Academic Press, Inc., 1974), pp. 89–125.

5 'Report of the Commission on the Measurement of Economic Performance and Social Progress', September 2009: www.stiglitz-sen-fitoussi.fr/en/index.htm.

6   See Chapter 5: 'Ireland's Well-Being at a Time of Change', in *Well-being Matters: A Social Report for Ireland*, Volume I, No. 119, October 2009: www.nesc.ie.

7   Standard Eurobarometer 71, fieldwork dates June-July 2009, published September 2009, http://ec.europa.eu/public_opinion/archives/eb/eb71/eb71_en.htm.

8   Detailed historical and comparative data – for Ireland and most other nations – is available at the World Database of Happiness website: worlddatabaseofhappiness.eur.nl/hap_nat/nat_fp.php.

9   'National Accounts of Well-Being: bringing real wealth onto the balance sheet', New Economic Foundation, 2009: www.nationalaccountsofwellbeing.org.

10 Alan Heston, Robert Summers and Bettina Aten, Penn World Table Version 6.3, online database, Center for International Comparisons of Production, Income and Prices at the University of Pennsylvania, August 2009: pwt.econ.upenn.edu/index.html.

11 Table 1.3 in 'Measuring Ireland's Progress 2008', CSO, 2009.

12 Nicholas Crafts, 'The Human Development Index 1870-1999: Some revised estimates', *European Review of Economic History*, 6, 2002, pp. 395–405.

13 Data from the 'Human Development Report 2009', UNDP, 2009 http://hdr.undp.org/en/statistics/.

14 Quoted in Rosemary Cullen Owens, 'Constance Markievicz's "Three Great Movements" and the 1916 Rising', in Gabriel Doherty and Dermot Keogh (eds), *1916 – The Long Revolution* (Mercier Press, 2007), pp. 197–224.

15 See Chapter 1: '1900–12' in Diarmaid Ferriter, *The Transformation of Ireland* (Overlook Press, 2007).

16 'From a Hermitage', October 1913, in *Collected Works of Pádraic H. Pearse – Political Writings and Speeches* (Maunsel & Roberts Ltd, 1922).

17 Joseph J. Lee, *Ireland 1912–1985: Politics and Society* (Cambridge University Press, 1989), p. 69.

18 Figures in a draft chapter on *Population and living standards in Europe 1870-1914*, by Leonid Borodkin, Carol Leonard and Jonas Ljungberg, published online, www.cepr.org/meets/.../Borodkin-Leonard-Ljungberg_Chapter.pdf.

19 Inequality of income distribution dataset, Eurostat, 2009: epp.eurostat.ec.europa.eu/portal/page/portal/eurostat/home.

20 Survey on Income and Living Conditions (SILC) 2008, CSO, November 2009.

21 Living conditions in 2008, Eurostat report 10/2010, January 2010.

22 P.H. Pearse, *The Sovereign People*, March 1916 in *Collected Works of Pádraic H. Pearse – Political Writings and Speeches* (Maunsel & Roberts Ltd, 1922).

23 Christopher T. Whelan and Richard Layte, 'Economic Boom and Social Mobility: The Irish Experience', Working Paper No. 154, ESRI, June 2004.

24 Joseph J. Lee, *Ireland 1912–1985: Politics and Society* (Cambridge University Press, 1989), p. 37.

25 P.H. Pearse, *The Murder Machine*, January 1916 in *Collected Works of Pádraic H. Pearse – Political Writings and Speeches* (Maunsel & Roberts Ltd, 1922).

26 Figure C1 in 'Key Data on Education in Europe 2009', Eurostat/Eurydice, January 2010.

27 *Ibid.*, Figure C10.

28 Detailed demographic information for Northern Ireland, including census results and more recent population trends are available from NISRA – the Northern Ireland Statistics and Research Agency: www.nisra.gov.uk.

29 *Belfast Telegraph*/Inform Communications opinion poll, March 2010, www.informcommunications.com/opinion-polls.aspx.

30 This poll dates to March 2010: http://www.belfasttelegraph.co.uk/news/local-national/belfast-telegraph-exclusive-poll-on-united-ireland-14721124.html.

31 Mick Fealty, Trevor Ringland and David Steven, *A Long Peace? The Future of Unionism in Northern Ireland* (pamphlet, 2003), p. 11.

32 Michael Collins, *The Path to Freedom* (August 1922, NuVision Publications LLC, 2005).

7   THE SUFFRAGES OF ALL

1 Cited in John O'Connor, *The 1916 Proclamation* (Anvil, 1999).

2 Quoted in Margaret Ward, 'Nationalism, Pacifism, Internationalism', in Anthony Bradley and Maryann Gialanella Valiulis (eds), *Gender and Sexuality in Modern Ireland* (American Conference for Irish Studies, 1997).

3 Rosemary Cullen Owens, 'Constance Markievicz's "Three Great Movements" and the 1916 Rising', in Gabriel Doherty and Dermot Keogh (eds), *1916 – The Long Revolution*, (Mercier Press, 2007), pp. 197–224.

4 Catriona Clear, 'Fewer Ladies, More Women', in John Horne (ed.), *Our War: Ireland and the Great War* (Royal Irish Academy, 2008), pp. 157–170.

5 Sara O'Sullivan, 'Gender and Attitudes to Women's Employment, 1988–2002', in Betty Hilliard and Máire Nic Ghiolla Phádraig (eds), *Changing Ireland in International Comparison* (The Liffey Press, 2007), pp. 135–162.

6 'That was then, this is now: Change in Ireland, 1949–1999', CSO, 2000.

7 Quarterly National Household Survey, Quarter 3, 2009, CSO, December 2009.

8 Ricardo Hausmann, Laura D. Tyson and Saadia Zahidi, 'The Global Gender Gap Report 2009', World Economic Forum, 2009: www.weforum.org/en/Communities/Women Leaders and Gender Parity/GenderGapNetwork/index.htm.

9 Detailed Irish results are available at the WEF website: www.weforum.

org/pdf/gendergap2009/Ireland.pdf.

10 Source: World Health Organisation Statistical Information System, 2005 data: www.who.int/whosis/en.

11 Seamus McGuinness, Elish Kelly, Tim Callan and Philip O'Connell, 'The Gender Wage Gap in Ireland: Evidence from the National Employment Survey 2003', The Equality Authority, 2009.

12 'The life of women and men in Europe: A statistical portrait', Eurostat, 2008.

13 'Euro Area Unemployment', Eurostat report 16/2010, 29 January 2010.

14 Live Register, January 2010, CSO, 3 February 2010.

15 Table 2.21 in Chapter 2, 'Report on Vital Statistics 2006', CSO, 2009.

16 'Marriages 2006', CSO, June 2009.

17 See: 'Married Life – The First Seven Years', Amárach Research, report published by ACCORD (Catholic Marriage Care Service), 2007.

18 'The Irish Study of Sexual Health and Relationships', Crisis Pregnancy Agency, October 2006.

19 Betsey Stevenson and Justin Wolfers, 'The Paradox of Declining Female Happiness', NBER Working Paper No. 14969, May 2009.

20 Michael Collins, *The Path to Freedom* (August 1922, NuVision Publications LLC, 2005), p. 75.

8   AUGUST DESTINY

1 From Parnell's speech in Cork, *Cork Examiner*, 22 January 1885: multitext.ucc.ie/d/Parnell_in_Cork_January_1885.

2 Chapter 25: 'Has History Any Meaning?' in Karl Popper, *The Open Society and its Enemies: Volume 2* (Routledge & Kegan Paul, 1945).

3 KOF Index of Globalization, Swiss Federal Institute of Technology Zurich, 2010.

4 'Redrawing the Map: Globalization and the changing world of

business', Ernst & Young, January 2010. http://www.ey.com/GL/en/Issues/Business-environment/Redrawing-the-map--globalization-and-the-changing-world-of-business---Five-business-responses-to-globalization.

5   Axel Dreher, 'Does Globalization Affect Growth?', *Applied Economics* 38, 10, 2007, pp. 1091–1110.

6   Frederick Turner, 'Abundance and the Human Imagination', *American Arts Quarterly*, Volume 25, Number 2, Spring 2008, http://nccsc.net/2008/5/22/abundance-and-the-human-imagination.

7   Daniel Taylor, *The Healing Power of Stories* (Doubleday, 1996), p. 20.

8   Stephen Kinsella, *Ireland in 2050 – How We Will Be Living?* (Liberty Press, 2009).

9   From Pearse's poem 'The Fool' available at www.irishcultureandcustoms.com/Poetry/PadraicPearse.html.

10 From Pearse's play 'The Singer': www.ucc.ie/celt/published/E950004-001/index.html.

11 From Chapter 11: 'Uprising', in Declan Kiberd, *Inventing Ireland – The Literature of the Modern Age* (Random House, 1995).

12 Quoted from 'The Soul of Man Under Socialism', in *The Complete Works of Oscar Fingal O'Flahertie Wills Wilde* (Collins, 1983).

13 For a useful introduction to his writings see Robert Coles (ed.), *The Erik Erikson Reader* (Norton & Co., 2000).

14 For an excellent insight into the history and legacy of the Irish missions, including the 1916 connection, see RTÉ's two-part documentary *On God's Mission*, first broadcast in March 2010: www.rte.ie/tv/programmes/on_gods_mission.html.